EMPOWERED BY
PRAISE

MICHAEL
YOUSSEF

CHARISMA
HOUSE

EMPOWERED BY PRAISE by Michael Youssef
Published by Charisma House
Charisma Media/Charisma House Book Group
600 Rinehart Road, Lake Mary, Florida 32746

Library of Congress Cataloging-in-Publication Data:
An application to register this book for cataloging has been submitted to the Library of Congress.
International Standard Book Number: 978-1-62999-988-3
E-book ISBN: 978-1-62999-989-0

While the author has made every effort to provide accurate internet addresses at the time of publication, neither the publisher nor the author assumes any responsibility for errors or for changes that occur after publication. Further, the publisher does not have any control over and does not assume any responsibility for author or third-party websites or their content.

21 22 23 24 25 — 9 8 7 6 5 4 3 2 1

Printed in the United States of America

To Dennis and Lavon Chorba
for their quiet yet powerful leadership
in the ministry of Leading The Way

CONTENTS

INTRODUCTION

THE EMPOWERING ADVENTURE OF PRAISE

THE WORLD HAS changed greatly in the twenty years since *Empowered by Praise* was first published. Here are just a few of the events that have shaken our culture over the past two decades: the September 11 attacks of 2001; the launch of Facebook in 2004, YouTube in 2005, and Twitter in 2006; the Arab Spring in 2010; the deaths of Osama bin Laden and Mu'ammar al-Gaddhafi in 2011; the rise of ISIS in 2014; the United Kingdom's Brexit vote of 2016; and the global COVID-19 pandemic of 2019–2021. In recent years smartphones, social media, and Zoom meetings have changed the way we relate to each other in business and at school.

Though it seems that the world has changed enormously over the past twenty years, these changes are minor and superficial compared with two great realities that never change: the reality of *God's* nature and the reality of *human* nature.

God's nature has not changed since time began. He's the same yesterday, today, and forever.

And human nature has not changed since the fall of Adam and Eve. We are still made in the image of God, still cut off from Him by sin, and still desperately in need of a Savior.

No matter how the world may change, this truth remains constant: God made us to know Him, to worship Him, and to give Him praise. We are made to experience and glorify the majesty of God.

Praise the Lord for His enduring truth!

A MIDDLE EASTERN VIEW OF PRAISE

If King David were here today, he'd shout to every believer, "Clap your hands! Make a joyful noise with musical instruments! Shout praises to the Most High, the almighty God!"

It's impossible to picture David standing quietly before us, droning theological platitudes. No! He would be excited. He would be dancing. He would shout and invite us to join him and all the saints in praising our Lord.

To our Western way of thinking, this seems way over-the-top. We believe in worship, but we don't want to seem overly emotional! Don't we sing hymns and praise choruses every Sunday morning? Don't we pray? Don't we give thanks and acknowledge God as Lord? Of course we do.

So what's all this fuss about praise?

It might help to look at this question from David's perspective—a Middle Eastern perspective.

I am by birth and upbringing a Middle Easterner, so I understand the passion of a man like David. In the Middle East you don't greet a friend with a casual hello. Even if you have just seen him the day before, you greet him heartily and even embrace him. Encountering a friend is a cause for gladness and celebration. Why? Because your friend is important to you.

How much more, then, would a Middle Easterner, a man like David, express his emotions upon encountering the Lord Most High! You can imagine that David's praise for God, his expressions of joy and gladness, would far exceed the greetings exchanged by two good friends.

King David, if he were here today, would urge us to leap to our feet with singing and dancing and shout, "Praise the Lord!"

How would you respond to the passionate, exuberant display of praise from King David? Would you dismiss him as a Middle Eastern religious fanatic? Would you tell him, "Sh! We don't allow noisy displays of emotion around here"?

Or would you gladly heed his call to praise God with your

entire being? Would you praise the Lord with all that you are, all that you have, and all that you will ever be, every day of your life?

THE NEGLECT OF PRAISE

Over the years, I've heard many Christians confess, "I don't praise the Lord as much as I should." It's true—none of us give God the intense, heartfelt praise He deserves. In fact, we should ask ourselves: "Do I praise God at all? Do I begin my prayers with praise—or do I jump straight to my list of requests? Are my prayers full of praise—or only petitions?"

I believe the church today is not a praising church because believers have not been taught the importance of praise. We don't realize that giving God the praise He deserves is vital to our spiritual growth. When we neglect praise, we block the channel through which God's power was meant to flow into our lives.

When C. S. Lewis was a new believer, he bristled at the Bible's command to praise God. He recalled his attitude at the time: "We all despise the man who demands continued assurance of his own virtue, intelligence or delightfulness; we despise still more the crowd of people around every dictator, every millionaire, every celebrity, who gratify that demand." It seemed to Lewis that the psalmists were trying to bribe God with praise: "More than once the Psalmists seemed to be saying [to God], 'You like praise. Do this for me, and you shall have some.'"[1]

But as Lewis grew in his faith, he learned that praising God really means *enjoying God* to the fullest. He wrote, "We delight to praise what we enjoy because the praise not merely expresses but completes the enjoyment....In commanding us to glorify Him, God is inviting us to enjoy Him."[2]

Many Christians view praise as something we do for God. They believe that when we praise God, we are doing something that benefits God. In reality, praise enables us to enjoy God. Praise prepares us to receive blessings from Him. Praise produces spiritual growth and development. Praise is the great "engine" that increases our faith as we pray and produces a more powerful witness in our lives.

If praise produces great benefits in the church and in our individual lives, why do we neglect it? Perhaps it's because praise doesn't fit into a simple formula. Praise is not a mere repetition of words, nor is praise a means of manipulating God into answering our prayer requests. Rather, praise flows from our love of God and our enjoyment of Him.

Praise is more than an obligation, more than a spiritual exercise. Praise is an empowering adventure. Praise leads us closer to the throne of God, to a more intimate relationship with our Creator, Savior, and Lord, and to a more fulfilling life on this earth.

LEARNING THE PRACTICE OF PRAISE

Praise is worthy of our attention. The Bible is filled with examples of God's people giving Him praise. It is also filled with commands that we grant the Lord the honor and praise that He alone deserves. Through this book I hope and pray that God will lead you on a life-changing experience as you learn how to praise God in all the ways Scripture teaches.

As I write these words, I pray that *Empowered by Praise* will do two things for you. First, I pray that it will send you to the Scriptures, hungry to find new truths about God and about the life of praise. I urge you to keep your Bible open as you read this book so that you might further delve into God's Word to confirm old truths and gain new insights.

Second, I pray that this book will motivate and inspire you to act on the truths that you learn, both from this study of praise and from your study of the Scriptures. Put the principles in these pages to the test by applying them to your own walk with the Lord.

Researchers have known for decades that if you give people information verbally, they will remember about 40 percent of what you've told them. If you show it to them visually, they'll remember about 60 percent of what they've seen. But if you engage people in *actively applying* what has been said and shown, they'll remember about 90 percent of what they've experienced.

So I pray that you will practice what this book teaches. Make full use of the study guide at the end of this book. After you read each chapter, spend time in reflection and prayer, and *actively apply* the suggestions that are offered.

If you practice and apply the principles in *Empowered by Praise*, you can be assured that you will grow in your relationship with the Lord. Great blessings will come your way, and you will live the Christian life with a sense of overflowing joy. Praising God does more than honor the Lord. Praise prepares you to enjoy His presence and experience His touch. A habit of praising God will enable you to grow strong in the Christian life.

As the world around us continues to change, make praising God the enduring centerpiece of your life. The Lord alone knows what the next twenty years will bring. But whatever our blessings, whatever our losses, whatever our sufferings, let us face them with confidence, courage, and hearts overflowing with praise and joy.

Let us join King David in proclaiming, "Praise the Lord!" Praise Him today. Praise Him as you've never praised Him before. Proclaim His glory to the heavens!

Praise the Lord!

PART I:

THE BLESSINGS
OF PRAISE

CHAPTER 1

PRAISE BRINGS GOD NEAR

A MAN STOOD IN a midweek prayer meeting I attended and began to pray, "O Lord, I will praise You with the instrument of ten strings." Just about everybody in the room opened at least one eye because we knew there were no musical instruments around when we started to pray. I could sense a feeling of bewilderment throughout the room. How was this man going to praise the Lord with a ten-stringed instrument?

Then the man continued his prayer. "I will praise You with my two eyes—I will look only to You. I will praise You by exalting You with my two ears—I will listen only to Your voice. I will extol You with the work of my two hands—I will work in Your service wherever You direct.

"I will honor You with my two feet—I will walk in Your statutes, and I will go wherever You lead. I will magnify Your holy name with my tongue—I will testify constantly of Your loving-kindness. I will worship You with my heart—I will love only You, and I will receive all the unconditional love You pour out in Your mercy, grace, and forgiveness.

"I thank You, Lord, for the ten-stringed instrument that You built into my being. Keep me in tune, and play upon me as You will. Ring out the melodies of Your grace. May the harmony of my praise song bring pleasure to You and glory to Your name. Amen."

This man knew about praising God with everything that was within him. We are to praise the Lord with our minds, offer praise from our hearts, and voice praise with our mouths. Praise involves the use of all that we have for God's glory.

Praise and the Meaning of Life

Every person I know, in the depths of his or her heart, seeks a life of fulfillment and joy. We are driven to know our reason for being. We want our lives to make a difference, to bring out something of lasting value.

As the saying goes, we don't want much; we want everything—at least everything that matters. To find a life of meaning, we need to concentrate on praising God. Not only does praise put us in closer communion with God; it also reveals things about ourselves. Praise opens our eyes to spiritual reality, to the love and power of God, and to our need for Him.

I have been a believer in Jesus Christ since I was a young man. I grew up in Egypt, singing songs of praise to God and hearing my mother and grandfather praise God for hours at a time. But even with such a consistent model of praise in my family, I still didn't grasp the true meaning of praise—that is, not until the spring of 1990.

My lovely wife, Elizabeth, had been experiencing some health problems. She went to the doctor, and after a careful examination he ordered a series of tests.

We were eager for a diagnosis, but the testing went on for some time. Finally, after a number of conflicting test results, a surgeon looked at me and my wife and pronounced one word that sent my stomach into convulsions and my heart into overdrive. You may have already guessed the word: cancer.

When we met with the surgeon, my wife was barely forty years old. My first thought was "God, she is too young to have breast cancer! How can this be happening?" My protest against God was a way of dealing with my fear. But then, in the midst of fear and the frustration that I could not take my wife's place or do anything except pray for and comfort her, I began to learn the power of praise. Our church was only three years old at the time, and our congregation was small. But we went immediately into intercession mode. We entered God's course of instruction, Power of

Praise 101, with the Holy Spirit and the Bible as our instructors. God began to take me and my family and our church through the first stages of learning what it means to praise Him in the midst of a storm.

The more we praised God, the stronger our belief grew that God was capable of all things. He is concerned about all the things that concern us, and He is infinitely compassionate toward His children. Praise refocused our fear and frustration. It changed our thinking and our feelings. The more we praised God, the deeper the fellowship we experienced with Him was. Even as my wife underwent medical treatment that brought physical healing, we underwent spiritual treatment that brought wholeness, hope, strength, and power to our souls. Our spiritual wholeness, and our experience of God's power, came through praising Him. Praise fully established the reign of God in our lives.

Ultimately praise reinforced the truth of who we are and who God is. He alone is the One who makes us whole. He alone is the One who walks through the valley with us, our faithful Lord who never leaves us or forsakes us. He alone is the source of all good things. Praise transformed our pain into victory.

Praise the Lord! Today my wife is in excellent health. We continue to praise God, not only for her healing but also for teaching us what it means to be empowered by praise to face any circumstance and any problem that life may hand us.

THE LIFE LESSONS OF PRAISE

Life rarely unfolds as we expect it to. Illness, personal loss, and financial setbacks can throw our lives off course. That's why praise is so important. Praise produces five major benefits in our lives. I like to think of these as the five Rs of praise. Praise *reveals* our true beliefs, and it *refocuses* our thinking and feelings. Praise is the *route* to deep fellowship with God, and it establishes the *reign* of God in our lives. Finally, praise *reinforces* the truth of who we are and who God is. Let's look at these essential life lessons one at a time.

Praise reveals our true beliefs.

The Scriptures tell us that our lips reveal whatever it is that we treasure in our hearts. (See Matthew 6:19–21 and 12:33–35.) Ultimately we cannot separate what we say from what we think and believe. Likewise, what we do—including our praise of God—is an expression of what we are inside. If we truly believe in God's goodness and His greatness, our belief will spill over into what we say about Him. We won't be able to hold back our praise. If we truly believe that God is the almighty King of the universe and the Lord of our lives, we won't be able to keep from expressing our praise to Him.

What we believe, we express. The strength and fervor, the depth and energy of our praise to God with our lips and our lives are directly proportional to our belief in God's goodness and greatness. Believing and praising build on each other. The more deeply and strongly we believe, the greater and more expansive is our praise. The more we praise the Lord, the more we behold His glory and see His hand at work continually in our lives. The more we praise Him, the more our faith grows and the more fervently and strongly we believe.

When my wife was diagnosed with cancer, my belief in God was tested. Was He a God of love, of healing, and of faithfulness? I had believed these things for most of my life, so I started praising God in advance for His care, His comfort, and His healing power. In praising Him, I grew to believe even more that He is exactly who He says He is.

Praise refocuses our thinking and feelings.

The world hassles us. I didn't have to tell you that—you already knew it!

Pressures and problems confront us every day. We seem to be continually dealing with sickness, death, trouble, suffering, and pain—if not in our personal lives, in the lives of those nearest and dearest to us. Even when we're not facing a major crisis, we must deal with the unavoidable difficulties of life—paying our bills, dealing with cantankerous people, coping with the challenges of our daily work, and responding to the many demands of those who are in authority over us.

And we must do all this while attempting to live out our faith in Christ Jesus. In this world we have to deal with very real fears, doubts, anxieties, and hurts.

But what happens to people who think about the problems and challenges of their physical lives only? Very soon the spiritual realm becomes misty, foggy, and unreal. The more we lose sight of God's realm, the more we become bogged down in the problems of earthly life. We slide into pessimism, cynicism, and depression. Life loses its luster, its joy, its excitement. Limiting our thinking to this world alone will grind us down into the dust from which we were created.

No matter how difficult or unjust our circumstances become, we can choose to serve God or to ignore Him. Likewise, by exercising our free will, we choose to praise God or to neglect the praise that only He deserves. We choose not only what we praise God for but how long we praise God, how frequently we praise God, and how intensely we praise God.

As I noted in the introduction, King David's life shows us that praise has a strong emotional dimension. But it is not driven by emotions; it is driven by our will. Praise must never be dependent upon emotions or whims. We must be careful never to say, "I prefer to praise God when I feel like it." We are to praise God in *all* situations, in both victory and defeat. We are to praise God when we're in need and when we're experiencing plenty.

A person can choose to praise God when he doesn't feel like it. In fact, it is precisely those times when it's essential that we praise God. The next time you are discouraged or despondent, start praising God. When you feel defeated or unable to break loose from addictions or bad habits, start praising God. When your marriage seems to be falling apart, start praising God. Why do I say this? Because praise is about what God desires to do, not about the power of your life circumstances. When you get your eyes off your immediate problem and put your focus on God, you redirect yourself—your mind, your emotions, your will— toward what God will do for you, not what man has done to you. At that point, God can step in and work in your life to produce real growth.

The truth for the believer in Christ is that this tangible, physical world is not the *real* world. The real world is our ultimate home—the heavenly spiritual realm where the presence of God permeates the atmosphere and where the power of God is openly manifested at all times. When we start to view our present physical life in light of the ultimate spiritual life, things begin to change.

Optimism, faith, and hope take root and flourish. Joy and peace grow in our hearts.

This is how praise refocuses our feelings. When we praise God, we are constantly reminded that He calls us to live and move in the world of the Spirit. Praise focuses our attention on the heavenly, spiritual reality of life. This world hassles us. God's realm comforts, empowers, and heals us. That's the *real* world we all seek.

Praise is the route to deep fellowship with God.

It is by means of praise that we more fully experience God's presence, both within us and at work all around us. The Scriptures tell us that God dwells in the praises of His people. He is the holy God "that inhabitest the praises of Israel" (Ps. 22:3, kjv). God pitches His tent wherever His name is exalted. The image painted by the psalmist is that God sits down and takes delight in the praises offered to His name. He camps out with those who acknowledge, glorify, and desire His presence.

If you are struggling with pain, sickness, or loss and are desperate for a sense of God's nearness, then start praising His holy name. As my wife and I struggled over the surgeon's diagnosis of cancer, we clung to God in praise of His love, His protection, and His faithfulness to us. We needed Him to set up camp amid our weakness and fear and suffering. And He did!

Friend, it is as we praise our Lord that we enjoy the warmest, deepest, fullest form of fellowship with our heavenly Father. No matter what you are facing, praise Him now.

Praise establishes the reign of God in our lives.

The simple fact of God's presence is this: wherever God dwells, God rules. He is our authority. He is sovereign over all. When we invite God to dwell in us, He reigns over our hearts. When we invite God to dwell in our marriages or our family relationships, God reigns over those relationships. When we invite God to exert His will and presence in our businesses, He reigns over our businesses.

Praise is our foremost means of inviting God to take up His residence with us and to establish His presence, authority, and purpose in every aspect of our lives. Since we all hunger for the nearness of God, let's look at four practical ways we can invite Him to set up camp in our daily lives.

We can praise God for His sovereignty.

God stays close to those who praise Him for His unlimited, all-loving ability to take authority over every area we yield to Him. A believer might pray, "Father, I declare that You are sovereign over my finances. I submit my will to Your will and ask You to help me in every financial decision I make. I want to make decisions that are pleasing to You."

The Lord has all resources at His command. He is the commander in chief of all forces that bring blessings our way. He established the law of sowing and reaping, the principles of giving and receiving (Gal. 6:7–10; Mal. 3:10). He can rebuke any force of evil that would attempt to steal from us, destroy us, or diminish us (Mal. 3:11–12).

In praising the Lord for His sovereignty over our finances, we are adjusting our own thinking and our emotional responses. Stock market forces aren't exalted as sovereign; God is. Employers and corporate downsizing aren't exalted as sovereign; God is. Economic slowdowns aren't exalted as sovereign; God is.

We can praise God for the guidance He gives in Scripture.

When we seek to yield an area of our lives to God's control, we immerse ourselves in both the commandments of God and the promises of God that are related to that area. We praise Him for giving us abundant promises in His Word as well as precise commandments to guide us. We thank and exalt God for working on our behalf, always conforming us to the likeness of Christ Jesus. (See Romans 8:28–29.) We praise Him for giving us the desire to change, the ability to change, and the strength to change. We praise Him because He has sent His Holy Spirit to dwell within us to help us change. He leads us to repent of our sins and to pursue a life of obedience. We praise God because He is always faithful to His Word.

In our example of praising God for His sovereignty over our finances, we might look up verses in the Bible that assure us of God's provision and then praise God for His specific promises to provide for us always.

We can praise God for His faithfulness as we obey His commandments.

In our example of praising God for His sovereignty over our finances, we might praise Him as we pay our bills. We would praise Him for giving us the provision of money to pay our financial obligations. As we give our tithes and offerings, we would praise Him for His promise to use our giving to grow our blessing. As we make our budgets, our investments, or our purchases, we would praise Him that He is helping us get out of debt, prosper in our finances, and become even more effective stewards of all He has given us. We praise Him because He is the Lord over all financial systems, all resources, all opportunities, all honorable work.

We can praise God for meeting our needs.

As God becomes sovereign over an area of our lives, we need to praise Him for the righteousness and goodness of the rule He has established. For example, if you have been praising God for His promised provision, make sure you also praise Him when

He brings financial recovery or blessing. "Lord, I praise You for bringing me to this place of blessing. I acknowledge that this is Your work and Your plan. I praise You for Your goodness toward me and my family. I praise You for showing me ways I can use the resources You have given me to have a greater impact in spreading the gospel."

Praising God leads to yielding our lives more completely to Him. And yielding to His authority then leads to greater praise. The more the Lord takes authority over any area of our lives, the more we see His hand at work in us and through us, and the more cause we have to praise Him. Praise feeds our obedience, and our obedience feeds more praise of Him.

Praise reinforces the truth of who we are and who God is.

An amazing thing happens as we praise God for all that He is and does. We see more clearly the truth of God's nature. We see that He is the unlimited, eternal, holy King. We see that He is all knowing, all wise, and all-powerful. We see His nature as loving, merciful, and long-suffering.

We also see more clearly the truth about ourselves, including the truth about our sinfulness. Let me openly confess that I have never come into the presence of God—praising Him, adoring Him, and honoring Him with the fruit of my lips—without also becoming more conscious of my own limitations, faults, and sins. The more we grasp all that God is, the more we must face all that we are not.

Someone said to me not long ago, "There's no mathematical equation to compare the infinity of God and the finiteness of man." How true! What fraction or percentage of God's power, wisdom, or love do we have? There simply is no way we can compare our weak, finite, limited existence with His vast and all-encompassing greatness.

When we come to God in praise and adoration, and if we are truly honest with ourselves, we become more conscious of our unworthiness. Even Job, a man so godly that God bragged about him, reached this same conclusion. When God revealed to Job His great power, Job replied in humility:

> I know that you can do all things; no purpose of yours can be thwarted....My ears had heard of you but now my eyes have seen you. Therefore I despise myself and repent in dust and ashes.
>
> —JOB 42:2, 5–6

We are like Job. No matter how righteous we are, seeing the glory of God confronts us with the tarnished, stained, dirty state of our own lives. Now, the reason for recognizing who we are is not so that we might walk through life with our heads hanging low. On the contrary! The purpose of our seeing the reality of our own sins and limitations is so we might repent of our sins and rely on God to be our source of strength. The more we see the dirtiness and weakness of our lives, the more we are to cry out to God to forgive us and to strengthen us by the power of His Holy Spirit!

Repentance and confession bring eternal benefits. The things that we confess to God now are things we will not have to face at heaven's judgment seat. Praise God because He gives us an opportunity to see our sins so we can ask Him to work in us to change us into the men and women we truly desire to become. The prayer of our hearts should always be, "God, make me into the person You want to live with forever!"

THE TRUE PURPOSE OF YOUR LIFE

One of life's great questions is this: "What is the purpose of my life?" To those who believe in Jesus as their Savior, the purpose of their lives is clear: we exist to bring glory to God. The apostle Paul wrote to the Ephesians:

> Praise be to the God and Father of our Lord Jesus Christ....
> For he chose us in him before the creation of the world to

be holy and blameless in his sight. In love he predestined us for adoption to sonship through Jesus Christ, in accordance with his pleasure and will—to the praise of his glorious grace....In him we were also chosen...in order that we, who were the first to put our hope in Christ, might be for the praise of his glory....When you believed, you were marked in him with a seal, the promised Holy Spirit, who is a deposit guaranteeing our inheritance until the redemption of those who are God's possession—to the praise of his glory.

—Ephesians 1:3–6, 11–14

These opening passages from Ephesians describe the purpose of life. We who believe in the salvation offered by the shed blood of Jesus Christ have been sealed by the Holy Spirit, and we now belong to Jesus. God has defeated the devil in saving us from the consequences of our sins. We are part of the inheritance of Christ Jesus—our very salvation brings glory to His name and to God's purposes on earth. Everything that He accomplishes in our lives is for our benefit, but it is also for His glory. As we pursue our life purpose in following Christ, our very lives are an expression of praise to God.

One of the most famous of all catechisms in the church proclaims that man exists "to glorify God, and to enjoy him forever."[1] To praise God is to enjoy God. If you were to ask the prophet Isaiah, he would tell you that God protects us and provides for us so we might proclaim His praise. (See Isaiah 43:20–21.) If you were to ask Peter, he would tell you that the purpose of suffering and trials is so that we might be refined and proved genuine in our faith and so that we may bring praise, glory, and honor to Christ Jesus (1 Pet. 1:6–7). If you were to ask Jesus, He would tell you that the purpose of everything God has created—including the stones of the earth—is to bring praise to God.

On the Sunday before His crucifixion, Jesus triumphantly entered Jerusalem as a great crowd shouted joyful praises to God: "Blessed is the king who comes in the name of the Lord!"

and "Peace in heaven and glory in the highest!" (Luke 19:38). The Pharisees admonished Jesus to rebuke the people. But Jesus replied, "I tell you...if they keep quiet, the stones will cry out" (Luke 19:40). Even God's creation exists to bring Him glory.

Jesus, who was present with the Father at creation, knew that the primary purpose of human life was to praise God and to enjoy fellowship with Him. If we fail to fulfill this purpose, the inanimate rocks will shout praises in our place. I don't know about you, but I certainly don't want a rock doing my job! Our proper response to all of life's experiences—both blessings and trials—is to praise God for what He has done, is doing, and will do in our lives and in the earth as a whole.

Your Unique Words of Praise

C. S. Lewis wrote, "Each of the redeemed shall forever know and praise some one aspect of the Divine beauty better than any other creature can. Why else were individuals created, but that God, loving all infinitely, should love each differently?"[2]

Praise fulfills part of your destiny as a uniquely created human being. Stop for a moment to consider this truth: nobody can praise God exactly the way you do, because no one else has had exactly your experiences. Nobody else has experienced the presence and power of God in exactly the same way you have. Nobody else will use the same combination of words and phrases and concepts to express praise to God. No one else will ever express the same praise in the same way to our great God.

Praise is a key aspect of the ultimate fulfillment of your destiny. Your praise to God is rooted in the very reason for your creation; it is an integral part of your purpose on this earth. So let praise flow freely from your heart, your mouth, and your entire being.

As a believer who knows God's love and blessing, praise the Lord today!

CHAPTER 2

PRAISE CONNECTS US TO HEAVEN

I OFTEN TELL PARENTS and grandparents that the greatest legacy they can leave their children is not cash, real estate, or stocks and bonds, but rather a heritage of love and devotion to Christ. I am among the most blessed of all people in this regard.

Because I left my home country of Egypt at a young age, I forfeited all material inheritance from my parents and grandparents. I inherited something far more valuable, however, than all the money in the world. I inherited my mother's model of intercession for the needs of others and her persistence in prayer. It was not unusual for my mother, Noza, to be in our family's guest room praying for one or two hours at a time. She developed this spiritual discipline of prayer and praise from observing her father.

My grandfather, Oza, was a building contractor by trade and a lay leader in the Brethren Church. When I was a boy, he lived in a small apartment adjacent to the home of my cousins. When I would spend the night with my cousins, I'd find myself waking up several times during the night. I have always been a light sleeper, and I soon discovered why I kept waking up. My grandfather was praising the Lord in an audible voice in his apartment next door. He seemed to praise God around the clock—several times a night at the very least.

I couldn't help but wonder why my grandfather was so full of joy. He had lost two sons when they were in their early thirties. He lost his wife while he was a relatively young man. Then later, at the age of eighty-eight, he lost his oldest daughter, my mother. Even so, until he died, at the age of ninety-two, he never ceased to praise God throughout the night and then again in the morning. I know now that it was praise, not life's circumstances, that gave my grandfather his heart filled with joy.

Growing up with this man's model of praise and devotion to God shaped my mother's life. And watching his life of joy had a permanent effect on my life.

Nothing the world offers could ever compare with this rich spiritual legacy.

Both my mother and my grandfather were committed to a life of praise. But for many believers today, such a lifestyle raises a basic question: Why should we praise God? Perhaps the foremost reason is one that was evident in the life of my grandfather: joy. We praise God as an expression of our joy in Him, and praising God in turn produces in us a life of deep and abiding joy. This is just a starting point, however. There are numerous reasons that we need to multiply our praise of the Lord.

Why We Praise God

The Bible is full of exhortations to praise the Lord. But besides being commanded to offer our praises, *why* are praise and worship so important? A nineteenth-century Christian answered the "Why worship?" question in this way: "We are forced by our very transformed nature in Christ not only to deal with this visible world but to relate to the heavenly world." Praise is what links us to God and to all His heavenly host—as well as to the saints of the past and to all living creatures that God created. Praise is the ultimate means of "networking" in God's kingdom!

Praising the Lord is the one thing we do on earth that we will do forever in eternity. There may be other things that will carry over, such as trusting, loving, and desiring God. But in our outward behavior, praise is the one thing we know with certainty that we will continue to do in heaven.

For the angels, praise is a full-time occupation. They are praising the Lord in myriad number even as you are reading this sentence. The Book of Revelation even records the content of their praise as they encircle Christ's throne:

> Worthy is the Lamb, who was slain, to receive power and wealth and wisdom and strength and honor and glory and praise!
>
> —REVELATION 5:12

And there's more. The angels fall on their faces before the throne and worship God with these words:

> Amen! Praise and glory and wisdom and thanks and honor and power and strength be to our God for ever and ever. Amen!
>
> —REVELATION 7:12

The angels, of course, are not the only creatures praising God in heaven. The saints who have gone before us—all people who have believed in Christ Jesus as their Savior and have served Him as their Lord—are joining the angels in this great praise song. Again, we read in Revelation:

> Before me was a great multitude that no one could count, from every nation, tribe, people and language, standing before the throne and before the Lamb. They were wearing white robes and were holding palm branches in their hands. And they cried out in a loud voice: "Salvation belongs to our God, who sits on the throne, and to the Lamb."
>
> —REVELATION 7:9–10

Our loved ones who have died and joined the church in heaven are worshipping God, praising God, adoring God—and doing so with utter abandon.

And the praise of God is not limited to angels and God's saints. The Bible tells us that all of the creatures and creation of God are joining in their respective languages of praise! The psalmist wrote:

> Praise him, sun and moon; praise him, all you shining stars.
> Praise him, you highest heavens and you waters above the
> skies....Praise the LORD from the earth, you great sea crea-
> tures and all ocean depths, lightning and hail, snow and
> clouds, stormy winds that do his bidding, you mountains
> and all hills, fruit trees and all cedars, wild animals and all
> cattle, small creatures and flying birds, kings of the earth
> and all nations, you princes and all rulers on earth, young
> men and women, old men and children. Let them praise
> the name of the LORD, for his name alone is exalted; his
> splendor is above the earth and the heavens.
>
> —PSALM 148:3–4, 7–13

What an unspeakably glorious praise song, coming from all creation and from the saints who have gone before, is filling heaven this very minute. I have no doubt that my grandfather and mother, as well as many others whom I loved and who died in the Lord, are part of that great praise choir! What joy to know that we who are in Christ Jesus will be praising God and adoring Him forever. Our bodies may be buried on this earth, but our praise will never die. It will go on forever.

It is baffling, then, that we who will be praising God on a full-time basis in heaven do so precious little praising of God on earth. Just look at the average church. There is the opening hymn, the closing hymn, and a choir performance in the middle. The rest of the service is devoted to preaching, taking an offering, making announcements, and other activities. As good as those activities may be, they should all flow from the praise of God. Praise should never be just "one of the things we do." Our praise on earth should mirror the praise of God that goes on continually and for eternity in heaven.

THE CHARACTER OF ETERNAL PRAISE

Let me point out three great attributes of our eternal praise. First, praise is to be corporate. Second, praise is to be unified. Third, praise is to be the atmosphere of our lives. Let's look at each of these characteristics.

Our praise should be corporate.

In the verses we looked at from Revelation, it's clear that the angels, the saints, and the many creatures of God are praising God as a group. There is no mention of individuals offering praise alone in heaven. The praise in heaven is corporate, and it is praise that is joined to the praise of all others who exalt God and proclaim Jesus as Lord.

Many Christians I know believe that praise is intended only for their private prayer closets or their personal worship. Not so! Our voices join with the voices of countless other believers on this earth to create a great outpouring of praise that flows upward to heaven. Our praise on earth becomes a part of the praise that is being offered to God in heaven.

Our praise should be unified.

Not only is the praise in heaven corporate, it is also expressed in a unified message. The angels, saints, and creatures of God are all "on the same page" when it comes to what they say in praise. We can make sure our own praise is unified with that of the heavenly host by taking care in how our praise is focused. The Book of Revelation provides several major areas on which to focus our praise:

The holiness of God

Around the throne of heaven are four "living creatures" who "day and night...never stop saying: 'Holy, holy, holy'" (Rev. 4:8). God is always and forever holy.

The omnipotence of God

In heaven, God is honored as "the Lord God Almighty" (Rev. 4:8). Heaven offers praise to God's "power and strength" (Rev. 7:12). God is not a "higher power"; He is the *highest* power.

God's eternal presence

The Lord is described in the praise songs of heaven as being the One "who was, and is, and is to come" (Rev. 4:8). He is also described as the One "who lives for ever and ever" (Rev. 4:9). God has no beginning and no end.

God our Redeemer

In Revelation we read that the creatures and the elders in heaven sing the following to the Lord Jesus: "You are worthy to take the scroll and to open its seals [thereby releasing God's judgment on the earth], because you were slain, and with your blood you purchased for God persons from every tribe and language and people and nation" (Rev. 5:9). God has redeemed us and made us a new kingdom to serve Him.

God our Provider

Scripture tells us that every good thing comes from God. He is the source of all wisdom, wealth, honor, and blessing. Again and again, we find the Lord acknowledged as the Source of all provision to us. The Lord is the Giver of "every good and perfect gift" (Jas. 1:17).

God our sovereign Ruler

One of the foremost things for which the Lord receives praise in heaven is for His rule and authority over this world and over the age to come. In Revelation 11:15 we read: "There were loud voices in heaven, which said: 'The kingdom of the world has become the kingdom of our Lord and of his Messiah, and he will reign for ever and ever.'" We are to honor God our mighty King, because He has won the battle against the enemy who seeks control over this earth.

God our Creator and Sustainer

The worshippers in heaven proclaim to the Lord: "You are worthy, our Lord and God, to receive glory and honor and power, for you created all things, and by your will they were created and have their being" (Rev. 4:11). As our Creator, the Lord knows every detail of our lives. He knows all our talents, abilities, and skills; our propensities, capacities, and desires. All these things have come from Him. He knows our personalities, our energy level, and our dreams. He is the author of our faith, having given to each of us a measure of faith to use to bring about His purposes on this earth (Heb. 12:2).

As our Sustainer, God is our Provider and our Protector. He is the One who gives seed to the sower and bread for our nourishment (2 Cor. 9:10). He is the One who defeats our enemies. He is the One who leads us to green pastures and beside quiet waters—both spiritually and physically—so that our souls are refreshed (Ps. 23:1–3). He is the One who rebukes the devourer for our sakes (Mal. 3:11, KJV).

Our response to all that God has done in creating and sustaining us is to say to Him, "You are worthy, Lord. I yield to You any glory, honor, and power that has come my way. I know that You are the source of it all."

For our praise of God to be unified with all the saints in heaven, we must be "on the same page," so to speak, when it comes to what we say to the Lord.

Listen closely to the words and music that you encounter at church. Is it genuine praise that flows with joy from the hearts of those around you? And is the message on the same page with the praises of heaven? Some of the "songs of praise" that we sing, I've noticed, are more about us than they are about the Lord. We tend to sing, "I will praise You," more than we sing, "Holy is Your name." We tend to sing, "I love You, Lord," more than we sing, "Thou art worthy to receive glory, and honor, and praise." Genuine praise is about God, expressed to God.

Our praise should be the atmosphere of our lives.

You can't read Revelation and not realize that praise forms the atmosphere of heaven. A saint can't breathe in heaven without breathing in the exhaled praises of others. Oh, that this may also be true on earth! Praise is to be the very atmosphere in which we live and move and have our being right here.

In an inspiring book titled *Early Christians of the 21st Century*, author Chad Walsh writes: "Millions of Christians live in a sentimental haze of vague piety, with soft organ music trembling in the lovely light from the stained-glass windows. Their religion is a pleasant thing of emotional quivers—divorced from the will, and divorced from the intellect, and demanding little except lip service to a few harmless platitudes."

He continues: "I suspect that Satan has called off his attempt to convert people to agnosticism. After all, if a man travels far enough away from Christianity, he may see it in perspective and decide it is true. It is much safer, from Satan's point of view, to vaccinate man with a mild case of Christianity so as to protect him from the real disease."[1]

Walsh has identified a pervasive problem among Christians. How are we going to get ready to praise God forever in heaven if we spend so little time praising Him on earth—not only in our congregational worship but also in our private times with God?

A veteran preacher, Jack Taylor, had this to say after years of preaching across the United States and around the world: "You may preach and plead with folks to repent, be cleansed, be committed, and follow the Lord, but few will make a lasting commitment without a prevailing atmosphere of praise."[2]

What is the atmosphere of your life? Do your words of praise line up with the worship of God in heaven? Are you involved in a community of believers that regularly and enthusiastically praises the Lord?

The faithful practice of true praise puts a person in direct line with all of the power available in heaven and on earth. A life of praise links us to God's eternal purpose and His perfect plan for us. It creates in us a landing pad for the angels of heaven to become our ministering servants. It establishes an environment that is creative, energetic, and evangelistic. It produces a community of faith in which needs are met and challenges are overcome.

So why don't we spend more time in praise to God? Why do we continue to struggle in our praise? We'll turn to that issue next.

PART II:

THE CHALLENGES OF PRAISE

CHAPTER 3

PRAISE DEMANDS
PERSONAL CHANGE

I F PRAISE CAME naturally, we wouldn't struggle so much over giving God the glory He deserves. If praise were easy, we would all be glorifying God throughout each day, and we would all be changed people as a result. In fact, that truth helps explain why praise is so difficult: praise demands that we make changes in our lives.

Most of us don't welcome the prospect of change. It's uncertain and unfamiliar, and it makes us uncomfortable. It's easier to try to avoid the challenges that come with change—even when that change is *guaranteed* to improve the quality of our lives.

The story is told of a woman who had developed hypochondria to a fine art. She routinely "suffered" from a variety of exotic ailments that seemed designed to win the attention and sympathy of others. One day two friends of this woman were conversing. One of them said, "Didn't the doctor give Eloise a new medication?"

"Yes," the second friend replied.

"Well, is she taking it?" asked the first friend. "Oh, no," the second friend said. "It might work!"

The good news is that praise *does* work to change us, and it changes us for good. It creates good attitudes, good outcomes in our relationships, and good desires. But God will not force them on us, even though they will improve our lives.

HOW PRAISE CHANGES US

God is eager to do good things in our lives, and it doesn't make sense that we would avoid His blessings. But our nature is such that we find comfort in what is familiar and tend to steer clear of uncertainty. Even though we know that God loves us, we still get nervous when we think about how He might want to change us.

When it comes to praise, there are certain things that won't stay the same if we start to faithfully glorify God in our lives. Here are five ways that God will work in us, to our betterment, if we develop a lifestyle of regularly praising the Lord: praise will transform our attitude, our energy level, our relationships, our spiritual perceptions and sensitivity, and our desires. Let's examine how praise brings about such dramatic changes in our lives.

Praise changes our attitude.

One of the foremost results of praise is that it changes a person's attitude. You cannot harbor anger, bitterness, resentment, or hatred toward others and genuinely praise God at the same time. A negative spirit toward others and positive praise to God simply cannot coexist.

Oh, you may start out your praise with something less than a joyful frame of mind. You may come to God out of obedience and begin praising Him without having a completely thankful heart. But once you start praising God, you cannot continue for very long without that negative spirit being broken. You cannot praise God consistently and deeply without the Holy Spirit breaking up your hatred and replacing it with the love of a loving God, shattering your anger and replacing it with the compassion of a compassionate God, destroying your bitterness and replacing it with the mercy of a merciful God.

I have seen this happen, over and over again, in my own life. No matter how bleak or sad my circumstances, I am lifted up in spirit as I praise the Lord. As I honor God for who He is and for the glorious things He has done, my own spirit is uplifted, and my eyes are opened to God's provision and blessing. I am 100 percent convinced that the best medicine for despondency and discouragement is praise. It is one of the keys to helping a person become whole after a great loss. It is the best "cure" for grief I have ever encountered.

Jesus affirmed the uplifting power of praise on the day He read from the Book of Isaiah in His hometown of Nazareth:

> The Spirit of the Lord is on me, because he has anointed me to proclaim good news to the poor. He has sent me to proclaim freedom for the prisoners and recovery of sight for the blind, to set the oppressed free, to proclaim the year of the Lord's favor.
>
> —Luke 4:18–19

Jesus then proclaimed that He was, and is, the full embodiment of this passage from Isaiah. He does the work of healing and transformation in us as we believe in Him.

This passage in Isaiah goes on to say that the Lord will "comfort all who mourn, and provide for those who grieve in Zion—to bestow on them a crown of beauty instead of ashes, the oil of joy instead of mourning, and a garment of praise instead of a spirit of despair" (Isa. 61:2–3). Notice the phrase "garment of praise"; it's important. Let me point out two things about a garment.

First, a garment is something you must put on. It does you no good if it is left folded in a drawer or hanging in your closet. You have to choose it, and you have to put it on. Likewise, nobody can do your praising for you. You must choose to praise God, and you must do the praising yourself. True praise flows from the heart. It is fed by your gratitude for God's provision and your understanding of God's greatness. The Lord gives us reasons to praise Him, He gives us a desire to praise Him, and He responds to our praises with rewards and blessings. But we must do the praising. We can put on the garment of praise and live wrapped up in God's joy, or we can refuse to put on that garment and lead a life of despair, discouragement, and fatalism. The choice is ours.

Here is the second important thing to notice. When God promises to provide us with a garment of praise, He contrasts it with a "spirit of despair" (Isa. 61:3). A spirit of despair in the Middle East, and especially at that time, led a person to tear his or her garments—literally to rip the fabric as a sign to the world of deep sorrow, a broken spirit, and feelings of being emotionally "undone" by intense sadness.

We see this repeatedly in the Old Testament. Tamar tore her ornamented robe in despair and heartache after her half brother raped her and then rejected her (2 Sam. 13:19). Job's friends tore their garments and sprinkled their heads with dust to commiserate with Job's great pain and suffering (Job 2:12). Ezra rent his tunic and cloak when he saw the unfaithfulness of the Israelites (Ezra 9:3). To rend a garment was to send a signal of a rent heart.

Not too long ago a woman shared with me that she had felt this type of overwhelming grief when she realized that her mother was dying from a stroke. "My hands instinctively went to my clothing, and I had a great urge to tear away my dress as a sign that my heart was breaking inside me," this grieving woman told me. "I was surprised at myself because I'm not normally a very demonstrative person. But my love for my mother was so great that this seemed to be the only way I could express my intense emotions. I didn't actually tear my dress, but I could understand for the first time why the people in the Bible expressed their sorrow and despair by rending their garments."

Thank God for replacing our spirit of despair with a garment of praise. The garment of praise is fresh, clean, and whole. What a tremendous picture of the work that the Lord desires to do in our hearts. Jesus wants to take away our sorrow and to cloak us with power, healing, and forgiveness. He wants to bring about our well-being, fulfillment, and joy. It is as we praise God that Jesus lifts the spirit of despair from us. We see beauty again. We feel gladness again. We feel peace and comfort again.

I recently heard about a grandmother who lost three of her grandchildren in a terrible house fire. Her daughter-in-law was also badly burned. The grandmother felt as if her own life was over and all was lost. She said to her pastor, "I didn't see any purpose in getting up in the morning. I knew I should want to be there for my daughter-in-law, but I just didn't have the strength to go to her bedside."

Then a wise friend said to this woman, "Get your eyes on Jesus. Start praising Him for who He is. Even if you don't feel like it, praise Him." The grandmother did start praising Jesus, because she didn't know what else to do or where else to turn.

"I didn't know what to praise Jesus for in the beginning," she said. "I turned to my Bible for the words of Jesus, and I'd read a passage and then say, 'Well, Lord, I praise You for saying that.' Occasionally I'd add, 'And I praise You for saying that to me right now.'

"I'd read about how Jesus healed somebody or cast demons out of somebody, and I'd say, 'Well, Lord, I praise You for doing that for that person who lived back in those days.' Then I started to add, 'And I praise You for doing that for people now.' Eventually I started to say, 'I praise You for doing that in my life today.'

"Some days, I must have praised Jesus for hours. I'd recall things I'd read in the Bible and praise Him while I was doing the dishes or running the vacuum. This went on for days and, eventually, for several weeks.

"Then one morning I awoke and looked outside. I thought for the first time in months, *What a beautiful morning!* It was the first time since the fire that I had seen anything in this world as being beautiful. Something seemed to crack open inside my dry old soul. The next day I found myself smiling at the antics of some neighborhood children attempting to climb a tree. It was the first time I had smiled in months. The next day I found myself baking a pie to take to my daughter-in-law, who was recovering from her burns and had returned home. It was the first time I had done anything for someone else in months.

"Day by day, week by week, the despair lifted. God directed me to a homeless shelter where I had countless opportunities to hug and comfort homeless babies and children while their mothers were working or seeking employment. God gave me back a purpose in living the more I kept my focus on Jesus.

"People say to me sometimes, 'Gladys, do you really believe Jesus healed people?' I tell them, 'Absolutely. I'm one of the people He has healed.'"

Any time you are feeling down, disappointed with life, or discouraged, it's time to start praising the Lord. Get your eyes off what you can't do, and fix your eyes on what God can do and what He desires for you to be. Get your eyes off your problems, and fix your gaze on what Jesus came to do in your life.

Praise will reverse your downward emotional spiral. If you don't feel a change after an hour of praise, then praise the Lord for another hour. If you need to, praise the Lord all day. If you need to, praise the Lord for hours at a time and for weeks at a stretch. Eventually a great breakthrough of joy will come to your heart. I have no doubt about it!

Praise changes our energy level.

Not only does praise change our attitude, it also changes our energy level. Have you ever been so emotionally exhausted that you could not sleep? Have you ever been so worn out by life's troubles that you couldn't rest? There is a weariness of the soul that exhausts us. And as much as that is true, there is also a joy that energizes us.

The prophet Isaiah wrote eloquently about this:

> Do you not know? Have you not heard? The LORD is the everlasting God, the Creator of the ends of the earth. He will not grow tired or weary, and his understanding no one can fathom. He gives strength to the weary and increases the power of the weak. Even youths grow tired and weary, and young men stumble andfall; but those who hope in the LORD will renew their strength. They will soar on wings

like eagles; they will run and not grow weary, they will walk and not be faint.

—ISAIAH 40:28–31

Isaiah tells us that those who hope in the Lord have their strength renewed and their energy restored. But how do we acquire real hope? We become hopeful when we look at what God can do, not what man has done. Hope wells up in us when we focus on the capabilities of God, not the weakness and inability of man. Hope springs up when we praise God for His perfection—recognizing and acknowledging and trusting in all that He is—rather than giving honor to the feeble attempts and less-than-perfect accomplishments of man.

If you are exhausted at the end of the day, shut yourself in for a while with God. Praise Him with every ounce of the energy you have remaining. I believe you will be refreshed, not only mentally and emotionally, but physically. There is a special strength that is imparted to those who praise the Lord. This kind of strength gives us the power to endure, to persevere, to outlast tough times. It gives us the power to intercede until God gives a breakthrough.

Praise changes our relationships.

Not only does praise change our attitude and our energy level, it also changes the atmosphere in our relationships. Try this. The next time you start to have a disagreement with your spouse or one of your children, stop and say, "Listen, we aren't getting anywhere by doing this. Let's try praising the Lord together." And then each of you begin to voice some of the reasons that you are grateful to God. Take turns voicing your praise for the many attributes and gifts and provisions of God—His strength, His love, His mercy, His forgiveness, His wisdom, and on and on.

Praise shifts the focus from pain to joy, from failure to hope, from fault to forgiveness. It's very difficult to remain at odds with a person over temporary human differences when you find yourself in agreement about the goodness and greatness of God. I'm not saying that praise cures problems in a relationship. But the mutual praise of God reestablishes a positive atmosphere in which two people can find God-honoring and mutually satisfying solutions to their problems.

Praise changes our spiritual perceptions and sensitivity.

In addition to changing our attitude, our energy level, and our relationships, praise changes our spiritual perceptions and sensitivity. Jesus repeatedly said to those who heard Him speak, "Whoever has ears, let them hear" (Matt. 11:15; 13:9). He admonished His disciples to keep their spiritual eyes open and their spiritual ears attentive. Praise opens our eyes and ears to God. When we focus on Him in praise, we are much more likely to hear what He has to say to us.

A mother, when she needs her child's full attention, often says, "Look at me." She knows that if the child looks anyplace else, he will be distracted and will be less likely to heed what his mother tells him. In this regard, we are a lot like children. We must keep our eyes on God if we are truly to attend to, and then follow, His commands.

Sometimes God's command is to change something in our life—to confess and repent of a sin or to make an adjustment in the way we are doing things.

Sometimes God's command is a sovereign word to us that results in emotional, spiritual, or physical healing. Sometimes God's command involves specific actions to be taken at specific times to establish or promote His purposes on earth. Sometimes God's command compels us to move to a deeper level of commitment or to move in a closer walk of faith. Whatever He wants to tell us, it will be easier to hear Him clearly when we are praising Him.

Praise changes our desires.

Even after all of those transforming blessings from God, there is still one more way praise changes us. It changes our desires. What is it that you deeply desire for God to do in your life? Answer that question and then ask yourself, "Did I come to that desire after praising God or before praising Him?" There is a huge difference in desires that are subjected first to a hearty dose of praise.

Some people seem to enter God's presence waving a long shopping list. They hardly greet the Lord before they move to their petitions, reciting all they want God to give them and do for them. They treat God as if He were some heavenly bellboy. I often say that people who come to God with a personal agenda are like those who go to a house, walk right past their host, head straight for the refrigerator to get out some food, then sit down to eat. Their wants drive their behavior. We wouldn't be that rude to our friends and neighbors, so how can we be that discourteous to almighty God?

THE TRUE PURPOSE OF WORSHIP

We have looked at five ways that praise changes us in dramatic ways. But the purpose of praise is not to get something from God. Rather, it is to put ourselves in a position to see God for who He is. We worship God not so much to do something for Him, although He does desire our praise, but to affirm His lordship over our lives.

The word *worship* comes from the word *worth-ship*, which means expressing to God the "worth" we place upon our relationship with Him. How much do you value what God has done for you? How much do you rely daily on what God promises to do for you? How much do you value or place worth on your relationship with Him?

Our beliefs about God are directly related to how we honor Him in our praise. For praise to deepen our devotion to the Lord, we need to examine not only how often we praise Him but also *how* we praise Him. The content, intensity, frequency, and duration of our praise reveal what we truly believe about God.

Examine the content of your praise.

What you believe about God is reflected in your praise. If you believe that He is your loving, patient, and forgiving heavenly Father, your praise will reflect those qualities of God. And if you truly see God as your loving Father, you will be eager to praise Him. On the other hand, if you believe God is angry and vengeful, just waiting to catch you in some mistake so He can punish and condemn you, then you will avoid praising Him. Why would anyone praise a supreme being who is petty and vindictive?

Your view of God determines your praise, and your praise mirrors your view of God. The degree to which you praise God and the things you praise God for indicate the degree of respect, reverence, trust, and awe that you have for God.

Your praise reflects the degree to which you value God in your life and the extent to which you fear Him.

I recently heard it said that "fear is never a good motivator." The speaker felt that it is better to tell a person about the love of God than to preach about the danger of going to hell. In my opinion, we need to preach both. We need to hold out the gracious love of God. We also need to tell people that to reject God's gracious, merciful love is to choose a life apart from God. And in eternity, our choice to live apart from God will permanently separate us from Him. I don't know of any definition of hell that is better than this one: "eternal separation from God's love."

When we do not fear God—when we do not have awe for God, respect for His authority, reverence for His presence, justifiable concern about the exactness of His justice—we make a grievous mistake. A healthy fear of God is one of the foremost motivators for a robust praise of God. God's holiness is not to be underestimated; His justice is not to be dismissed; His patience is not to be tested. When we have a proper sense of awe and fear of God, we will want to praise Him with all our being.

When we come face to face in the praise of someone who is more beautiful than anything we'll ever behold on earth, the awesome King of the universe, we too are likely to find ourselves without adequate language. God's character is far beyond our ordinary experience. He really is holy. He really is the Maker of all things, the judge of all people, the ruler of all nations.

God's greatness might make the language of praise more difficult, but it's also what makes praise necessary. We need to acknowledge and revere who God is. Praise brings us to a fuller recognition of God—not so we might cower before Him, but so we might bow before Him in humble worship.

Examine the intensity of your praise.

The degree to which you see God as being not only able but eager to meet your needs is likely to determine the intensity of your praise. If you do not see God as being bigger than your problems, then why bother to seriously praise Him? If you see God as capable of meeting your needs but unwilling to act on your behalf, you are likely to praise God with a "divided mind." Your mixed emotions toward Him will produce a halfhearted faith and a reluctance to trust Him fully.

In contrast, if you see God as not only capable of dealing with your problems but fully willing to move heaven and earth on your behalf, your praise will be enthusiastic and heartfelt! Those who see God as being on their side, working always for their eternal benefit, are those who praise God with the most intensity and the greatest amount of faith.

The magnitude of a person's need often leads to greater intensity in his praise. Those who have been delivered from much are likely to be far more vocal and far more emotionally intense in their praise. In contrast, those who have never faced suffering, or have never trusted God to meet a desperate need in their lives, are likely to be far more lukewarm in their praise.

Examine the frequency of your praise.

The extent to which you see God intimately involved in every detail of your life will be reflected in the frequency of your praise. If you believe that God cares about you every moment and in every circumstance and that no situation is beneath His notice and His care, then you are likely to be praising God all the time! "Praise the Lord" will be something you say, in one form or another, countless times throughout the day. On the other hand, if you believe God only cares about the major moments in your life or that God is a remote, unconcerned observer of your life, your praise of Him is likely to be far less frequent.

Examine the duration of your praise.

The depth of your relationship with God is likely to reflect the amount of time you spend in praise. If you know the Lord well—not only in length of years but in depth of trust and degree of reliance—you are far more likely to spend longer periods of time in praise. You have a greater understanding of God's nature, and you have far more experience with His work in your life. But if you have not cultivated your relationship with the Lord, you are likely to find that five minutes in praise feels like five years. You don't know God well enough to spend more time with Him.

Part of what influences our personal relationship with God is the degree to which we are grateful for the Lord's mercy to us and especially the degree to which we are thankful for our salvation. If you are deeply grateful that God has saved you from the consequences of your sin, you will have so much praise that you cannot express it all in just a few moments. Your praise will be overflowing because your gratitude is so great. By comparison, those who are not sure they are saved, who feel that God "owed" them salvation, or who have allowed their salvation experience to grow cold are likely to spend very little time in praise.

Praise reveals the heart of our relationship with God, our view of Him, and our level of trust in Him. Praise also works mighty changes in us, touching our attitude, our energy level, our relationships, our spiritual perceptions and sensitivity, and our desires. Praise opens us up spiritually to hear God's commands. In other words, praise helps us see ourselves, and God, more clearly, and it changes us in very fundamental ways. It takes courage, my friend, to make such changes. It takes courage to reexamine what we believe to be true about our Father, His only Son Jesus, and the Holy Spirit.

Take time now to look at your life of praise. Examine the content, the intensity, the frequency, and the duration of your praise. Then ask yourself, "Am I ready to be changed and challenged by focusing my life on praising God?"

I urge you to accept the challenge. Don't fear the changes that praise will bring, but instead embrace God through praise and look forward to the wonderful work He wants to do in your life as a blessing of praising Him. Start devoting more time and intensity to praising God, and then prepare to be transformed by Him.

CHAPTER 4

PRAISE TOUCHES DEEP EMOTIONS

A LITTLE GIRL ONCE asked her grandfather, "Grandy, why do your eyes fill up with tears sometimes when you look at me?" Her grandfather replied, "Oh, honey, those aren't tears. That's liquid love!"

Oh, that our tears might flow freely as we offer praise to God! He is worthy of all expressions of our love, including our expressions of deep emotion.

In considering the reasons that it is difficult for us to live a life of praise, we must consider the challenge of honestly expressing our emotions to God. People often limit the work of God in their lives because they do not want to reveal certain aspects of their personality or emotions to Him. It is our natural tendency to try to hide from God due to the sinful pride that we inherited from Adam and Eve. The truth, of course, is that God already knows everything about us.

Pride also causes us to be concerned about how we appear to others. We worry that other people might see us cry or become overly enthusiastic as we praise the Lord. We don't want to appear too emotional or too "fanatical." We fear that humbling ourselves before God in praise might make us appear weak, dependent, or even overly spiritual. This is especially true if we think others may hold our faith against us. Being thought of as overly religious could cost us a promotion at work, or it might lead to our being excluded from the social circle we aspire to. We are so worried about our image that we hesitate to freely praise God with all our heart.

What is amazing to me is that we do a pretty good job of

expressing exuberant emotions in nonreligious settings. Watch any major sporting event, and you'll see people who are nearly jumping out of their skins with excitement over a touchdown or a grand-slam home run. We also do a fairly good job at expressing our disappointment or sadness. Even men are beginning to learn that it's all right to cry when they feel sadness, rejection, or inner pain. I didn't say we're completely there yet, ladies, but we men are starting to show our emotions more.

But what about showing our emotions when it comes to God? What happens to our genuine enthusiasm and joyful, loving expressions of gratitude in response to the Lord's goodness in our lives? This type of emotional expression is still rare in many churches and in the lives of many, many Christians.

Can you imagine how the world at large—or for that matter, the church at large—would respond to King David, who danced openly through the streets of Jerusalem on the day the ark of the covenant was finally brought into the city? Let's examine our own views on praise as we take a look at this story of heartfelt, unselfconscious praise to the Lord.

A King's Model of Praise

After David had been sworn in as the ruler of the people by God's anointing and God's calling, one of his first executive orders was to bring the ark of the covenant to Jerusalem. The ark, which at that time represented the presence of God, had been taken captive by the Philistines, who had subsequently released it when they experienced great plagues that they attributed to it. After being loaded onto a cart drawn by oxen, the ark had made its way to Kiriath Jearim, where it remained for some time in the keeping of a man named Abinadab.

David's first attempt to bring the ark to Jerusalem had ended in disaster. The ark had been loaded onto a new ox-drawn cart with two men named Uzzah and Ahio guiding it. Once underway, one of the oxen stumbled and Uzzah reached out to steady the ark. As soon as his hand touched it, he died. The ark was then taken aside to the house of Obed-Edom while David and the priests tried to understand what had happened. Why had touching the ark wrought such immediate and devastating results?

David returned to Jerusalem and pitched an open-roof tent to house the ark. He summoned the high priests and commanded them to consecrate themselves and then return to the place where the ark had been left. They were to bring it to Jerusalem by carrying it on their shoulders with poles, just as the Lord had commanded Moses. David then appointed the leaders of the Levites to appoint singers "to make a joyful sound with musical instruments: lyres, harps and cymbals" (1 Chron. 15:16). As part of the ark's return, a sacrifice of seven bulls and seven rams was to be made.

Musicians were assembled, sacrifices were made, and the day of the ark's return was scheduled. On that day, the Bible says that David and the elders brought up the ark "with rejoicing"— with great shouts and songs and a clamor of praise. In one account of the procession, we read this description: "Now David was clothed in a robe of fine linen, as were all the Levites who were carrying the ark, and as were the musicians, and Kenaniah, who was in charge of the singing of the choirs. David also wore a linen ephod. So all Israel brought up the ark of the covenant of the LORD with shouts, with the sounding of rams' horns and trumpets, and of cymbals, and the playing of lyres and harps" (1 Chron. 15:27–28). What a parade this was!

And notice who was dancing and rejoicing more than all the others. It was King David. We read in 2 Samuel 6:14 that David was "dancing before the LORD *with all his might*" (emphasis added). David was so overcome with joy and emotion that he danced and leaped and shouted and sang with abandon. He didn't care what others thought of him—he was overflowing with the joy of the moment.

The ark was coming to Jerusalem. God's presence was with

him, never to leave him. God's power was with him, always to uphold him.

David had no solemn words for such a moment; there simply were no words to convey all that he wished to express. He was so joyous that he could not keep his feet from skipping, his arms from waving, his voice from shouting and singing, or his hands from clapping. What his words could not fully express, his actions did in praise to God.

How would we react to a leader today who displayed such emotion before the Lord? Would we wonder about his stability, asking if he had what it really takes to lead the people?

No matter what those around David thought, we know that he was concerned about honoring God, not impressing those around him. And if God is honored by our expressions of praise, what other opinion counts?

David's emotional celebration took place before "all Israel" (2 Sam. 6:15). But today, I find that many Christians are intimidated by corporate praise. They are uncomfortable in a congregation that is praising God with deep fervency of spirit and great joy of expression. Some are even uncomfortable with the idea that they might voice aloud their praise to God in the quiet solitude of their own homes, in their cars, or while they go for a walk. Why are we afraid to praise God openly and with our emotions?

I asked this very question recently, and someone answered me: "It's embarrassing." When I asked, "Why is it embarrassing?" he could give no response other than to blush.

Now before you decide that I'm out of line for suggesting that we lose ourselves in praising the Lord, take a moment to reflect honestly on your own relationship with Him. Begin by reflecting on your private prayer life. How much time do you spend honoring, adoring, worshipping, and praising God? What percentage of your prayer time is devoted to voicing thanksgiving and honor to God?

I am convinced that those who spend very little time in prayer, and specifically those who spend little of their prayer time in praise, adoration, and worship, are those who are most uncomfortable in corporate settings where praise is being voiced. Jesus said, "Then you will know the truth, and the truth will set you free" (John 8:32). When you really know the truth of Jesus, you can't help but praise Him. When you start praising Him, you can't help but want to praise Him even more. And when you praise Him a great deal—when praise becomes the most extensive aspect of your private prayer life, when praise flows from you naturally—you won't be the least bit intimidated by other believers around you who are praising God. Those who are embarrassed or intimidated by the praises of others tend to be those who are not accustomed to praising the Lord on their own. My prayer for you is that you will be set free to praise the Lord with a full range of your emotions.

BIBLICAL EXPRESSIONS OF PRAISE

In chapter 2 we looked at descriptions of heavenly praise from the Book of Revelation. We saw that angels, saints, and "creatures" in heaven all join in praise by singing and by declaring God's glory. The picture of heavenly praise is one of movement, of involvement, and of loud exclamation. There is no sense that the angels stand sedately, with hands folded, and sing their praise in barely audible voices. In fact, the Bible's portraits of praise—from both the Old and New Testaments—show us that praise is an active expression of worship.

Praise is "noisy."

The Bible usually describes praise in an active voice—verbal and vocal. And it is sometimes loud. Psalm 66:8 admonishes, "Praise our God, all peoples, let the sound of his praise be heard." Psalm 66:1 increases the volume by declaring, "Shout for joy to God, all the earth!"

Praise is accompanied by movement.

As we read descriptions of praise in the psalms, we often see references to physical motions such as bowing, clapping, dancing, or raising one's hands. Psalm 66:4 says, "All the earth bows down to you; they sing praise to you, they sing the praises of your name." Psalm 63:4 says, "I will praise you as long as I live, and in your name I will lift up my hands." The uplifted hand is a silent declaration: "I love You; I rely on You; I exalt You; I salute Your greatness." It's a symbolic way to submit our will and our ways to the will and ways of God.

But can clapping or shouting by themselves be an act of praise? Yes! Psalm 47:1 tells us, "Clap your hands, all you nations; shout to God with cries of joy." Many times we are moved beyond words to express our joy or enthusiasm for God's greatness. At those times, a shout of joy or the sound of our clapping hands might be the best expression of what's in our heart.

Of course, not all noise and clapping qualifies as praise. Not all shouts are expressions of exaltation to God. But our loud, glad expressions to the Lord, coming from hearts overflowing with wonder at God's goodness, can be an act of worship.

In addition to shouts and clapping, there is the dance of praise. Psalm 149:3 refers to this: "Let them praise his name with dancing and make music to him with timbrel and harp."

Praise involves many postures.

There are times when praise is less exuberant but still involves action.

Throughout the Scriptures we find examples of men and women who fell on their faces before God as an act of worship. In the Middle East the prone position is one of utmost honor and respect. It's a posture that says very clearly, "I humble myself out of my great respect for you." Lying prostrate before God tells Him that we're ready to serve Him.

Oftentimes I find myself in the most authentic and deepest form of humble worship and exaltation of God as I fall on my face, prostrating myself fully before the Lord with my face to the ground. I have never made a major decision in my ministry without coming in humility before the God of all the earth with my face to the ground.

In 2 Chronicles 20:18 we read that King Jehoshaphat "bowed down with his face to the ground, and all the people of Judah and Jerusalem fell down in worship before the Lord." In the aftermath of this expression of deep humility, some of the Levites then "stood up and praised the Lord, the God of Israel, with a very loud voice" (2 Chron. 20:19).

The king praised God while lying facedown; the Levites stood to offer praise to the Lord. You can praise God standing, sitting, kneeling, or lying in your bed at night. You can praise God while walking or taking a morning jog through the neighborhood. There is no single correct posture for praising God. For our praise to be authentic, however, we need to seek a posture that fits the condition of our heart.

Praise is accompanied by song.

While it's true that the position of our body says something about the way we are praising God, the posture of praise is joined by the words we utter and how we utter them. At times, our words of praise are best set to song. The psalmist wrote: "Praise the Lord. Sing to the Lord a new song, his praise in the assembly of his faithful people" (Ps. 149:1). "Sing the glory of his name; make his praise glorious" (Ps. 66:2).

Praise is accompanied by musical instruments.

Sometimes I wish I were gifted in the area of playing music. When I read the psalms, I see the lists of musical instruments that are used in praise to our Lord. Psalm 150 must certainly be considered the "instrumental music psalm":

> Praise him with the sounding of the trumpet, praise him with
> the harp and lyre, praise him with timbrel and dancing, praise
> him with the strings and pipe, praise him with the clash of

cymbals, praise him with resounding cymbals. Let everything that has breath praise the LORD. Praise the LORD.

—PSALM 150:3–6

Praise is accompanied by tears.

The church I pastor in Atlanta, Church of the Apostles, grew from a handful of members to more than two thousand in less than fifteen years. In that time, many people have visited our church. Many of them stay, some come only once, and a number attend for some time, leave, and then return. In fact, a number of people have said to me, "I left the Church of the Apostles for a while, but now I'm back. And I didn't really like coming back."

That admission, of course, always raises my curiosity. So, I ask them why they came back if they don't like it. Their response: "I find myself crying when I come to the Church of the Apostles." To that I answer, "So do I. Join the club!"

When we praise God as a congregation, we often cry in His presence. The reason for our tears is not sadness or guilt or any form of inner pain; rather, we are crying for joy. A heart that has been transformed by God and is lifted up in praise is nearly always going to leak a little in the form of tears. At times, we simply cannot contain all that we feel toward God—our thanksgiving, our awe, our enthusiasm, and our wonderment go beyond mere words. At those times, our joy finds expression in tears.

THE FREEDOM OF PRAISE

God seeks believers who will praise and worship Him in freedom. We should not try to mimic a certain style or tradition; we should instead praise God in the way that expresses to God the fullness of who we are. We need to worship God in the freedom of the Holy Spirit, which includes the freedom to stand, sit, kneel, raise your hands, shout, cry, dance, or clap. It includes the freedom to worship with great motion and noise and exuberance, and it also includes the freedom to worship with tears and silence and awe.

The apostle Paul told the Christians in Galatia that "it is

for freedom that Christ has set us free" (Gal. 5:1). This is not a freedom that gives us license to do anything we want to do, but rather the full freedom to serve Christ with all of our being—body, mind, and spirit. We are not to use our freedom to "indulge the flesh; rather, [to] serve one another humbly in love" (Gal. 5:13). We are to use our freedom to express ourselves in praise and worship—thanking God for all that He is and does in us, and for the love, joy, peace, patience, kindness, goodness, faithfulness, and gentleness He has shown to us and is manifesting through us to others. We are to embrace the Lord in praise with our entire being, with no part of our being held back.

Within the wide latitude God gives us for praise, one aspect of our worship is constant: we must maintain a prevailing attitude of deep respect for the Lord. We worship the Lord in awe. We come to Him to voice our praise with a deep awareness that He knows everything about us and yet He still loves us. Genuine praise and worship is not a matter of the words spoken or the posture taken or the instruments played as much as it is a matter of the heart.

We worship God in reverence. We worship God with the fullness of who we are. We worship God with a humble heart that is willing to fall prostrate before Him—no matter who may be watching. Christ has set us free, and we are to worship God in freedom.

Don't hesitate any longer. Go ahead and praise God freely, with all of your being, today.

CHAPTER 5

PRAISE CALLS US TO BEAR WITNESS

A S WE HAVE already seen, praise changes us. It affects us personally and corporately—altering our attitudes, our spiritual sensitivity, our heart's desires. And we have seen the way praise challenges us to be open before the Lord. But the changes don't stop there.

Praise also changes our witness to others. It accomplishes this by changing who we are and enhancing and enlarging the reflection of Christ in us. Praise expands our ability to proclaim whose we are.

Whenever we praise God, we are challenged to express God's goodness to others. Praise is not for our own benefit alone. It spills out of the church into the world. It becomes a key element in our witness of Christ Jesus.

When we make a habit of praising God, we discover that we cannot keep quiet about God; we have to tell others about His goodness and greatness.

However, when opposition arises in response to our witness, we may be tempted to go back to our former habit of neglecting to praise God. If that has happened to you, I encourage you to open the floodgates of praise in your life once again!

ADORING AND EXTOLLING THE LORD

There are two words in Scripture that are often linked to praise: *adoration* and *extolling*. Adoration is "thinking" about the goodness and greatness of God. Quiet, adoring meditation on the wonderful works of God should be part of our daily worship. In fact, in the

Scriptures, adoration is often called "meditating upon" the Lord. A wonderful work happens in us when we spend time adoring God. A quiet, "settled" contentment fills us and strengthens us.

Extolling, on the other hand, is telling others about the goodness and greatness of God. Our quiet adoration is directed to God, but when we praise God in the presence of others—when we tell others about the great, wonderful, awesome things that God has done and about the majesty of His presence—then we are extolling God.

In this regard the psalmist wrote:

> Every day I will praise you and extol your name for ever and ever. Great is the LORD and most worthy of praise; his greatness no one can fathom. One generation commends your works to another; they tell of your mighty acts. They speak of the glorious splendor of your majesty—and I will meditate on your wonderful works. They tell of the power of your awesome works—and I will proclaim your great deeds.
>
> —PSALM 145:2–6

The purpose of our extolling God's greatness is so that others might celebrate His work on earth. In response to our praise, the psalmist noted, "they celebrate your abundant goodness and joyfully sing of your righteousness" (Ps. 145:7).

In Psalm 126 we see that even among the gentile nations, the people who were outside the realm of God's chosen people, it was said "the LORD has done great things for them" (v. 2). After hearing God's people extol God in joy and laughter, the hearers were led to praise God themselves.

How can we extol God today? It starts with a recognition of His work among us. When we extol God's goodness, we are not telling others what we wish God would do, but rather what He has already done. We are not trying to work up a feeling; we are responding in honest wonder and gratitude for the great things we have received.

What is it about extolling God that causes others to grant

Him honor? It has to do with the genuine spirit with which we offer our praises. Note the progression: God's work and abundant blessing produce genuine joy and gratitude in our hearts that, when expressed openly by God's children, penetrate the hearts of others.

It is ironic that the call to extol God before others would discourage some Christians from making a habit of outwardly praising the Lord. A lifestyle of extolling Christ Jesus actually brings great reward, so why wouldn't we want to make this a priority in our lives?

Once we are born again and receive a new spiritual nature in Christ, we become citizens of two realms—the natural, physical world that we live in daily, and the spiritual, heavenly realm in which we will live eternally. What we say and do on this earth is recorded in heaven's annals. What we say about the Lord is echoed throughout all eternity.

Jesus made this clear when He said, "I tell you, whoever publicly acknowledges me before others, the Son of Man will also acknowledge before the angels of God. But whoever disowns me before others will be disowned before the angels of God" (Luke 12:8–9). It's clear that what we say to the Lord and what we say about the Lord are vitally important.

As you consider the seriousness of this statement, ask yourself what Jesus is saying about you right now to His holy angels. It shouldn't be hard to answer this question, since it is directly related to what you are saying about Jesus to those around you and to the Lord Himself.

A PERSONAL PRAISE SONG

As I stated earlier, in chapter 1, nobody can praise God exactly as you can. Your praise to the Lord is unique, and so is the witness that you bear to others when you extol the goodness and greatness of God.

King David gave us one of the greatest praise songs of all time.

He sang this song the first time when he extolled God's greatness after the Lord delivered him from his enemies, including the hand of the murderous Saul. As you look at the content of David's song, notice the characteristics of his praise to God.

Praise is a personal statement.

David's song to God, recorded in 2 Samuel 22:2–51, is highly personal. He referred to God Almighty as "my God" (vv. 3, 7). David described God's faithfulness and protection in vivid images, characterizing the Lord as my rock, my fortress, my deliverer, my shield, and my salvation (vv. 2–3). He went on to describe God as "my stronghold, my refuge and my savior" (v. 3). It's clear not only that God was very personal to David but that God's work in David's life was very real to the king.

David didn't sing a praise song filled with generalities. He used very specific language:

+ "He drew me out of deep waters" (v. 17).

+ "He rescued me from my powerful enemy, from my foes" (v. 18).

+ "The LORD turns my darkness into light" (v. 29).

+ "It is God who arms me with strength and keeps my way secure" (v. 33).

+ "He trains my hands for battle; my arms can bend a bow of bronze" (v. 35).

+ "You exalted me above my foes; from a violent man you rescued me" (v. 49).

David was convinced of God's presence, His power, and His answers to prayers for help and deliverance. Our praise should reflect the same confidence in a miracle-working God. Our praise of God should be as personal and as specific as David's was.

A bishop once said to me, "You talk about Jesus as your personal Savior and your personal Lord as if you 'own' Him. You speak of Him as being 'your God,' just the way a person speaks of owning a car."

I replied, "Oh, no. I don't call Him my Savior and Lord because I think I own Him. I call Him my personal Savior and Lord because I know He personally owns me."

Praise recognizes God's work in others.

Although David's praise of God was highly personal, it was not exclusive. David believed that what God had done for him, God did also for others. In 2 Samuel 22 he lists God's mighty works on behalf of others:

"To the faithful you show yourself faithful, to the blameless you show yourself blameless, to the pure you show yourself pure" (vv. 26–27).

"You save the humble, but your eyes are on the haughty to bring them low" (v. 28).

"He shields all who take refuge in him" (v. 31).

David knew he had not cornered the market on God's blessing. It is this balance between knowing what God has done for us and knowing that God desires to do the same for others that keeps us from becoming proud. Our praise should honor God's work in the lives of all people.

Extolling God for His Future Work

We are called not only to extol God for what He has already done but also to proclaim the wonderful works that God will do in the future. We praise God with the faith and confidence that what He has promised He will bring to pass.

"But," you may ask, "how can I know what God will do?" The quick answer is "because He has already told us." There are two things you can count on God doing in you and in the life of every believer. He has promised to conform you to the likeness of His

Son. He has also promised that you will receive everlasting life and live with Him forever in heaven.

God will conform us to Christ Jesus.

How do we know that God will, without a doubt, conform us to the likeness of His Son? Here is what the apostle Paul assures us in the eighth chapter of Romans:

+ God is working all things to our good (v. 28).

+ He is conforming us to the likeness of His Son (v. 29).

+ He is justifying us and one day will glorify us (v. 30).

+ He is enabling us to be conquerors over all troubles and hardships (v. 37).

+ He is never going to be separated from us or deterred from His work in us—not by anybody or anything (vv. 38–39).

+ His motivation for doing all of this on our behalf is love (vv. 37, 39).

God is at work in my life, and He will never cease to be at work in your life, not for any moment during the remainder of your earthly life and then on into eternity! My friend, if that doesn't make you want to stand up and shout praises to God, I don't know what will! You have a bright and glorious future. You have every reason to be filled with hope. God is for you, so nothing can stand against you. And He is at work turning everything in you and around you to good. He is making and remaking, fashioning and refashioning, molding and remolding, renewing and then renewing again all things in your life so you truly are a completely new creation, one that He looks upon just as He looked upon the world in the opening days of creation and said, "It is good."

You can praise God with full confidence today for the work

He will continue to do in you now and in eternity. You can extol God to others to build up their faith and their expectancy about what God will do in their lives too. What God has promised He will accomplish!

God will give us a home in heaven.

Jesus said, "My Father's house has many rooms; if that were not so, would I have told you that I am going there to prepare a place for you? And if I go and prepare a place for you, I will come back and take you to be with me that you also may be where I am" (John 14:2–3). This is not speculation; this is a promise.

I find it very easy to praise God for providing a glorious place where I will spend all eternity. Some people argue that heaven is a state of mind, nothing more than an abstract idea. Others claim it is nothing more than wishful thinking or a figure of speech. I want to tell these pessimistically miserable people, "Jesus never spoke of heaven in a figurative sense. He spoke of heaven as being a literal place—a place He came from, a place to which He was returning, and a place to which He would one day take us. I choose to believe in what Jesus said about heaven."

Heaven is a real place, with real joy, real peace, and real worship, and it's my real home. During my life, I have lived in Egypt, Australia, and the United States. But heaven is my permanent address. Praise the Lord for His promise of eternal life!

Benjamin Franklin wrote as his epitaph, "Like the cover of an old book, its contents torn out, lies here food for the worms. But the work shall not be lost. For it will appear once more in a new and more elegant edition Revised and corrected by The Author!"[1]

Think about the heavenly realm that we will enjoy forever. We will have new bodies, free of all pain, disease, disfigurement, and limitation. In heaven we will experience no sorrow, no suffering, no tears. We will be with saints who love and praise the Lord as we do, with no separation by race, tribe, language, or culture. All who believe in Jesus Christ will join in singing the same hallelujah choruses! In heaven we will join the saints and countless angels in the worship of God. We will be in the immediate presence of the Lord Jesus Christ, and we will have uninterrupted fellowship with God our Father.

But that's not all. In heaven we will be free forever from temptation and sin.

We will experience all of God's abundance and beauty. We will know exceedingly great joy beyond anything we currently can imagine. In heaven we will experience what it means to "rule and reign" with Christ Jesus. You can praise God with full confidence in the place He has already prepared for you and in the eternal life you will enjoy in His presence.

When believers extol God for His promise of eternal life, the saints of the church are refreshed. Plus those who are lost will feel conviction. If they desire to know God, they will feel motivated to repent of their sins and receive God's forgiveness. When believers extol God, they create a hunger in others to enter into the fullness of eternal life.

If people do not desire to know God, they may reject us, but when that happens, we can still rejoice. Extolling God enlarges the understanding of others about Him. No matter what decision they make, God is working.

Spend time adoring the Lord quietly today. Then, after adoring Him in private, openly extol His greatness and goodness to others. Give those around you an opportunity to come to know the God who blesses every believer with His promises, His presence, and His eternal glory. In that way, you will double the blessing.

CHAPTER 6

PRAISE WARS AGAINST
OUR PRIDE

Aman came up to me recently and asked, "Dr. Youssef, have you ever been through a wilderness experience—a real desert time?"

"Yes," I said. "Have you?"

"Yes," he replied. "It lasted almost a year. I just couldn't feel God's presence. I felt dry inside. I didn't have any enthusiasm for the things of God. It was all I could do to get up on Sunday mornings and get to church. And then, about three months ago, things changed."

"What happened?" I asked.

"Well," he said, "I asked myself, 'What's different in my life between now and the time I first came to the Lord?' I started thinking, 'Back then, I trusted God for everything. I could hardly wait to see what He would do next. I praised God for everything that happened—every new insight I had into the Bible, every opportunity I had to witness, every blessing I received.' That's when I realized that now I was doing things on my own strength."

"So what did you do?" I asked.

He said, "I got down on my knees and told the Lord I was a failure. Doing things on my own didn't work. I started praising Him for everything, trusting Him for everything. And it was as if the heavens opened up and started raining on my desert. I came alive again in my soul."

Then he laughed. I said, "What's so funny?"

"I just realized something," he said. "I came alive in my soul at the same time I died to myself!"

This man's desert experience had brought him to a life-changing insight, a principle we see throughout Scripture: New life comes from death. Spiritual vitality comes from putting away selfish desires. But the blessings of God don't come without a cost. To enjoy a life of blessing, we must set aside the self-directed life that serves our own interests.

THE SIN OF PRIDE

Satan works overtime to get us to hold on to our pride, because that is the one thing that will prevent us from enjoying God's blessing. Satan knows that praising God wars against our pride and helps us submit ourselves to God's rule. Since praise is our ally in the battle against pride, Satan uses pride in several forms to make it difficult for us to practice a life of praise.

How does Satan talk us into neglecting praise? He begins by distracting us: God doesn't need our praise; our time is better spent on other things; other people are taking care of praising God, so we should focus on more "important" things. To prevent us from directing our praises to God, Satan even tempts us to practice self-praise—words that appeal to our vanity and words intended to pump up our ego and inflate our sense of self-importance.

I am not saying that speaking positive words or thinking positive thoughts about ourselves is always wrong. We are admonished in Scripture to exercise the spiritual gifts that God has given us, and to help us identify those gifts, we need to take an honest look at ourselves and our abilities. As we do this, however, we are to exercise "sober judgment" (Rom. 12:3; see also Romans 12:6). In our positive thoughts about ourselves, we are never to diminish the primary importance of praise to God.

Satan tries to convince us that pride is harmless, that it is nothing to be concerned about. The truth is that pride is deadly. It destroys not only our relationship with God, but it also destroys our relationships with other people. It is devastating to a person's emotional health, and ultimately, it can kill the body. King Uzziah was a powerful, prosperous king who did a great deal of good for the nation of Israel. He was a man whom the Lord had greatly blessed. But the Bible tells us that Uzziah's pride led to his downfall (2 Chron. 26:16). He took upon himself privileges in the temple that were not rightfully his, and as he raged against the priests before the incense altar, he broke out in leprosy. This man who had been king was then shunned by all as a leper. Uzziah was forced to live in a separate house until the day he died (2 Chron. 26:19–21).

Pride is deadly, which is why we need the healing and protection that come through the praise of our Lord. Praise unmasks pride. It reveals pride for the deadly cancer that it is. Either pride will stop the flow of praise from a person's lips, or praise will uproot and defeat pride.

However, before we can attack the presence of pride in our lives, we must be able to identify the forms it takes. That means we must be able to detect the lies that Satan tells us. First, he makes us believe that God favors us more than others. Second, he convinces us to remove our emotions from our expressions of praise. And finally, he causes us to value our self-image more highly than authentic praise that honors God. To enter the life of praise, we must recognize these lies and take action against the pride that lies behind them.

Satan's lie about favoritism

There is a form of pride that I call "grace pride." Grace pride says that because of God's abundant blessings on my life, I must be more spiritual and more favored by God than my fellow Christians. People with this kind of pride think God loves them more and regards them more highly than others because He has allowed them to receive an abundance of material riches or social influence.

Several years ago, a very dear friend of mine—a man who was almost like a father to me—went to be with the Lord. He was a very wealthy man, yet he lived far more modestly than most. He used to say that those who have been highly blessed by God need to remind themselves—even more often than those who are needy—where their blessings came from. There is no question about the Source of our blessings. James told us clearly: "Every good and perfect gift is from above, coming down from the Father of the heavenly lights" (1:17).

Without this reminder from Scripture, the blessed person can easily start to think he earned God's favor in some way. Humility tells us the truth that God has no favorites. He has only sons and daughters, and He favors them all. His blessings to us come from His love and grace, not because we are "special." If we have any economic or social or political influence, it is only because of the Lord.

Satan's lie about emotions

Not only does the devil prompt us to consider ourselves more favored than others, he also influences us against expressing our full emotions in praise to God. Although we dealt in chapter 4 with the emptying of our emotions before God—our laughter and tears, our celebration and reverent awe—let me explain why the devil fights so hard to keep us from praising God with our emotions.

As we grow into adulthood, we tend to equate maturity with a lack of outward emotional expression. As children we are allowed great freedom in expressing our emotions, but when we grow up, we are expected to keep our feelings hidden. Adults learn not to cry, not to laugh uproariously in a way that would attract attention, and not to do anything that might seem abnormal in light of the cultural norm. We are expected to face the most difficult circumstances of life with a stoic attitude that conveys, "I'm in control. This doesn't faze me a bit." Those are lies of Satan.

The truth is that we are not in control; God is. So our attempts to convey the image that nothing bothers us means we have bought Satan's lie.

The truth is that God created us with emotions, and our

emotions help us empty ourselves before the Lord. That's another reason Satan opposes our emotional demonstrations of praise. Outward expressions of praise—laden with emotion—are the most powerful means of emptying all of our inner self to God. There are times we should allow ourselves to cry until there are no more tears, laugh until we can hardly breathe, and praise God out loud until we have no more voice. It is then that we are fully empty of self—as one person said, we come to the dry end of ourselves—so that God can fill us with His presence, His love, and His Spirit.

When we come before the Lord to praise Him in humility, we must lay down our pride. Praise requires us to say to the Lord, "You are everything, and all belongs to You. All that I am, have, and will ever have or be, I yield to You." That is when the Lord begins to build us from the bottom up. Ultimately, praise changes the landscape of our heart and mind. It renews us. And that, my friend, is a process the devil detests.

Satan's lie about self-image

Perhaps the most persuasive lie, the one that is easiest to fall for, is the pride attached to self-image. We don't want others to see us as a "religious nut." Religion in moderation is socially acceptable. But faith that moves us to bold expressions of praise and devotion is just too much. After all, we have an image to maintain.

One of the most obvious displays of pride in opposition to praise was that of Michal, the wife of David. I shared in chapter 4 the story of how David danced before the Lord with utter abandon as he and the elders of Israel brought the ark of the covenant to Jerusalem. The Scriptures tell us that Michal, daughter of Saul and wife of David, was watching this procession from a window. "And when she saw King David dancing and celebrating, she despised him in her heart" (1 Chron. 15:29).

She had chosen not to join in the celebration, and upon watching the king lose himself in praise to the Lord, she chose to express her displeasure. Michal was waiting for David when he returned home. You can almost hear the cynicism in her voice as she ridicules her husband: "How the king of Israel has distinguished himself today, going around half-naked in full view of the slave girls of his servants as any vulgar fellow would!" (2 Sam. 6:20). She was upset that David had taken off his royal robes and had chosen to wear the same garment as every other man in the procession. In other words, she was upset that he had humbled himself before the Lord and presented himself, not as king of Israel, but as a common man.

Why would Michal be so upset over something her husband did? It all gets back to pride. She felt that her sense of dignity as queen had been violated. She was concerned about what others would think and say and how her reputation would be damaged. The simple fact is this: She was too proud to have done what David did. I can imagine her telling David that he didn't know how to be a king because he was just a kid from the country who didn't know court protocol. It is clear that she considered his behavior to be vulgar, common, and beneath her. Michal's pride prevented her from participating in the praise of God, and it kept her from enjoying the blessing that comes as a result of praise.

David's response to God was just the opposite. Protocol was the least of his concerns. He knew he belonged to Yahweh and that was all that mattered. He was acting to please God, not man. He said to Michal, "It was before the LORD, who chose me rather than your father or anyone from his house when he appointed me ruler over the LORD's people Israel—I will celebrate before the LORD. I will become even more undignified than this" (2 Sam. 6:21–22).

Undaunted by his wife's rebuke, David basically told her, "You ain't seen nothin' yet! No one is going to keep me from honoring God with all that I am and all that I have. No matter what praise may cost me in terms of reputation, I will abandon all before the Lord."

How many people today are more concerned about appearances than about having a heart that is completely devoted to

God's praise? When our self-image restrains our praise, we see pride at work.

The Sin of an Untrue Heart

Pride is not the only sin that kills praise. An untrue heart also squelches both our desire and our ability to praise God. An untrue heart is a heart that is insincere, hypocritical, or filled with doubt. Hebrews 10:22 tells us, "Let us draw near to God *with a sincere heart* and with the full assurance that faith brings" (emphasis added). We can honor God with our lips but still harbor bitterness, hatred, or deep anger in our heart. We can sing hymns yet deep down inside be determined to live an immoral lifestyle. We can mouth the words of a personal testimony yet hold in our heart something that is not pleasing to God. We may try to draw near to God with our words yet restrain our heart from genuine intimacy with our heavenly Father.

Jesus said to the Pharisees, who were careful to keep all of the man-made laws while neglecting God's requirements, "You hypocrites! Isaiah was right when he prophesied about you: 'These people honor me with their lips, but their hearts are far from me'" (Matt. 15:7–8). It is possible to have confession without commitment. It is possible to fool others and even to fool ourselves when it comes to praise. But it is never possible to fool God. He hears the hidden meaning behind our words. He knows the intent, motives, and desires of our heart. For praise to be acceptable to almighty God, our heart must be true.

When the Bible speaks of the heart, it is referring to the totality of our inner being—the intricate combination of intellect, emotional response, and will. For our praise and worship to be acceptable to God, our intellect, emotions, and will must all line up with God's plan. They must all be submitted to Him.

You may be thinking, "Well, then, I don't have a chance when it comes to practicing the life of empowering praise. My intellect, emotions, and will often move in the very opposite direction of

God's plan." My friend, don't be dismayed. God never intended for you to conform to His will on your own. That's why He sent His Holy Spirit to give you the grace and power to live a righteous life. God desires to do this work in you—that's the very essence of His grace.

In his book *How to Worship Jesus Christ*, Joseph Carroll makes the point that "God's Holy Spirit within you will help you meet God's demands."[1] God has never made a demand on us that He has not covered by His own provision. His Holy Spirit nudges, prods, molds, and fashions us so that our hearts are true—so that our thoughts line up with our words, our words line up with our behavior, our motives and desires and plans line up with God's commands.

The Bible gives us a wonderful picture of a believer's total submission of intellect, feelings, and will to the commands of God. Abraham submitted his entire being to God when he was asked to sacrifice his son Isaac. This story is a compelling demonstration of a follower of God surrendering his entire being to the will of God.

The surrender of intellect

Abraham's obedience to God required that he submit his intellect. God told him to sacrifice his son Isaac as a burnt offering (Gen. 22:1–2). This command defied all understanding, logic, and reason. God had already said that Isaac was the son of promise, the child through whom Abraham would bless the world. How could Isaac fulfill this great destiny if he was sacrificed? It didn't make sense, but Abraham surrendered his intellect to God and placed Isaac on the altar.

The surrender of feelings

God asked Abraham to surrender not only his intellect but also his feelings. Throughout Genesis 22 we find a deeply personal and emotional description of the relationship that Abraham had with Isaac. For Abraham to actually bind his son to an altar stacked with wood and to raise a knife against him must have been the greatest emotional agony a human could know. God asked Abraham to sacrifice the son of his old age, the one person on earth whom he loved more than any other. It didn't seem loving, but Abraham surrendered his emotions to God and obeyed.

The surrender of will

Abraham was asked to surrender a third part of his being, his will. All of his heart resisted the idea that he was to sacrifice his son. Nevertheless, Abraham surrendered his will to God and obeyed.

God continually puts His servants in a position that requires a choice on their part: Will they say, "My will over Yours," or will they say, "Not my will, but Thine"? Jesus could have called on the angels of heaven to rescue Him, but instead, He submitted His intellect, His emotions, and His will to the Father, saying, "My Father, if it is possible, may this cup be taken from me. Yet not as I will, but as you will" (Matt. 26:39).

Likewise, Abraham surrendered his desires, his reason, and his will to God, and he did so with faith. A true heart is a "sincere heart *and with the full assurance that faith brings*" (Heb. 10:22, emphasis added). Abraham fully expected God to raise Isaac from the dead if he sacrificed him. He expected God to be true to His promise that He would bless the earth through Isaac. Abraham knew that the Lord would stand by His promise. Abraham had faith that God would receive the glory and honor due His name. He had banished pride by abandoning his own preferences and submitting fully to the goodness and wisdom of God.

A Personal Decision to Surrender

The decision to surrender all of your life and to have a true heart before God is a solitary, individual decision. Only you can yield your all to Christ. Abraham did not even tell his wife, Sarah, what God had commanded. I have wondered what I would do in such a situation. Would I tell my wife what God had asked of me? Would I be willing to act without gathering Christian brothers around me to offer their prayers and advice? I feel certain that if Abraham had consulted anyone else about God's command, he would have been told, in so many words, "Abe, you're getting old. You're not thinking clearly. Surely God doesn't want you to do this. You're hearing a voice, all right, but it's not God."

I am not at all suggesting that it is wrong to get godly counsel when seeking the will of God. But in the end, we personally are responsible for surrendering fully to all that God asks of us. We must obey God as He directs us.

Many years ago, the Lord laid a heavy call on my heart to begin a new congregation in Atlanta. I admit that I argued with God about His call. I said, "Lord, I already have an international ministry. I have opportunities to preach Your Word around the world. Anyway, what if I try to start a church and fail? What will my enemies say? And how can an Egyptian who looks like me and talks with my accent start a church in Georgia? I won't fit in!" God's call defied logic; it challenged my emotions; it confronted my will.

I called a group of Christian brothers together and told them what I believed God was asking me to do. Not one of them thought it was a good idea. To a man, they thought launching this church wouldn't work. After our meeting, I felt exhilaration that my good Christian, God-fearing brethren had not confirmed this call. This was just the excuse I was looking for!

Then, as I drove away from that meeting, the Spirit of God within me said in very blunt terms, "When did I ask you to check with somebody else?" What my counselors and I thought "felt right" wasn't at all what God commanded in my life. I had one choice, to start a church in Atlanta, Georgia. I thank God every day that I chose to obey. To have disobeyed would have been the end of my ministry—I have no doubt about that.

God expects our surrender to Him to be total. God expects

our surrender to Him to be daily. God fully expects our surrender to Him to be a sacrifice.

In the psalms praise is mentioned in the context of sacrificing to God (Ps. 27:6, KJV). The writer to the Hebrews made the connection even more clear by using the expression "sacrifice of praise" (Heb. 13:15). Praise is a sacrifice because it costs us something. It costs us our pride and our self-made, self-serving plans. Praise requires that we lay ourselves down on an altar before the Lord and say, "I yield to You every aspect of my life—all my talent, all my possessions, all my dreams and goals, all my relationships. I give them all to You."

I encourage you to pray this prayer today:

> *Lord Jesus, I surrender my intellect, I surrender my emotions, and I surrender my will. Lord Jesus, Help me surrender daily. Help me obey You daily that I may worship You with a true heart. Amen.*

The Elements of Genuine Praise

Praise is difficult because it compels us to open ourselves up to God in new ways. It requires total submission and costs us our devotion to self. But the empowering benefits that come from praising God are so wonderful that the cost becomes insignificant in comparison to all that we receive.

Before we can receive those empowering benefits, however, praise must become more than a mere desire of the heart. It must become something we practice with consistency. "But how?" you may be asking.

In the next section, we will examine in practical ways how we can approach God in praise. What are the elements of genuine praise? What words do we say before the Lord? As we will see, there are four vital elements of genuine praise.

PART III:

THE ELEMENTS OF PRAISE

CHAPTER 7

PRAISE FLOWS FROM A THANKFUL HEART

Henry Frost experienced God's blessing on his mission work in China. The Lord allowed him to have a great impact on that nation. In his biography Frost told of learning an incredible lesson related to the power of praise.

One day the missionary received tragic news from home, and a dark shadow covered his soul like a blanket. Even though he prayed diligently, the darkness did not lift. Instead, it deepened as the days passed.

Then the day came when Frost drove to one of the inland mission stations and saw a message written on a wall: Try Thanksgiving. At that moment he turned his prayer to praise and thanksgiving, and as he did, the shadow of darkness lifted and never returned.[1] Let's learn an important lesson from Henry Frost and try thanksgiving!

One of the most joyful passages in the Bible is a psalm that calls us to thanksgiving:

> Shout for joy to the LORD, all the earth. Worship the LORD with gladness; come before him with joyful songs. Know that the LORD is God. It is he who made us, and we are his; we are his people, the sheep of his pasture. Enter his gates with thanksgiving and his courts with praise; give thanks to him and praise his name. For the LORD is good and his love endures forever; his faithfulness continues through all generations.
>
> —PSALM 100

If you ever question for even a moment how to praise God, turn to Psalm 100. In a context of thanksgiving, this short psalm covers all the basics of praise. The psalm tells us:

The Lord is God! He is our Creator and our caring Shepherd.
The Lord is good. The Lord is loving. The Lord is faithful.

Notice that in the midst of praising God, the psalmist tells us to "enter his gates with thanksgiving" (v. 4). In the Middle East, the "gate" of a home was located on the street. In many neighborhoods in my native country, Egypt, this is still the case. Just inside the gate would be a courtyard, and beyond the courtyard would stand a door or entryway into the person's dwelling—or in the case of this psalm, the "court" of our great King.

Why should we be thankful as we enter the Lord's "gate"? In biblical times, the gates were opened only to friends, relatives, and those who were well known to the occupant of the dwelling. Once inside the gates of a home, a guest was afforded hospitality, and beyond hospitality, protection. He was greeted and treated as if he were a member of the family.

It makes sense, then, to express gratitude for such treatment. As we enter the Lord's gates, it is necessary to express thanksgiving to our Host:

"I am so grateful, Lord, to be within the protection of Your dwelling place. I am so grateful to partake of the provision that You offer me."

"I am so grateful to be separated from the grime and troubles of the world's highways and to spend time in Your presence, Lord. I am so grateful that You are the refuge to which I can turn."

"I am so grateful to have the opportunity to come to You openly and to communicate with You freely. I am so grateful for the privilege of having unhindered fellowship with You."

Truly, the praise of God grows out of a thankful heart. When we consider everything that God has done for us, and everything

He continues to do for us each day, we should never run out of things to thank Him for. The psalmist tells us:

> Let them give thanks to the LORD for his unfailing love and his wonderful deeds for mankind. Let them sacrifice thank offerings and tell of his works with songs of joy.
>
> —PSALM 107:21–22

Our thankful praise to the Lord should reflect that He gives us the very breath we breathe, He governs the beat of our hearts, He upholds our strength, He heals our bodies and minds and emotions, He saves our souls, He provides for our needs, and He defeats our enemies for His glory. When we give thanks, it's as if we are offering a sacrifice to the Lord. It is a sacrifice of our words and the time that we spend in thanksgiving, and it is even more a rending of the heart so that we truly feel thankful. In offering a sacrifice of thanksgiving, we acknowledge our neediness even as we recognize and acknowledge God's abundant supply. We admit our limits as we praise our limitless God.

Without gratitude as our attitude, our words of praise are hollow and void of deep meaning. Throughout the psalms, we find a great emphasis on having a thankful heart.

"I will praise God's name in song and glorify him with thanksgiving" (Ps. 69:30).

"I will sacrifice a thank offering to you and call on the name of the LORD" (Ps. 116:17).

"Sing to the LORD with grateful praise; make music to our God on the harp" (Ps. 147:7).

GRATITUDE IS AN ATTITUDE

Have you ever knocked yourself out for someone, really given your all to make sure he or she had everything necessary for success? Have you ever done that and then received absolutely nothing in return, not even a word of thanks?

Have you ever been in a relationship in which you were always the giver or the doer and all the other person did was take, take, take? Have you ever seen people who were truly blessed in every way, and yet all they talked about was what was wrong in their life and how victimized they have been?

Have you ever loved and loved…and had your love taken for granted or even rejected outright?

If you have had any of these experiences, you understand how Jesus must have felt. Many times, Jesus gave and gave, and the crowd took and took, and then they came back the next day for more. They came to Him to get something for themselves but never responded with thanksgiving for His blessings.

It's not only the people in Jesus' day, of course, who treated Him this way. If we honestly allow God's mirror to reflect our inner attitude, we will be shocked to discover how few of us have really developed an attitude of gratitude toward our Lord.

I once heard about a man who sat down to a meal with his family. He bowed his head and prayed: "Lord, we are truly thankful for this food You have provided to us." Then, as the meal continued, he berated the cooking, complained about the coffee being cold and the bacon being too crisp, and criticized the way the eggs were cooked. His young daughter asked, "Dad, do you think God heard what you said when you prayed?"

The father replied with confidence, "Certainly!"

She pondered his answer and then asked, "Dad, do you think God heard you complaining about your bacon and coffee and eggs?"

The father replied, "Why, of course. God hears everything." She then asked, "Which do you think God really believes?"

A Lesson in Gratitude

In Luke 17 we find a tremendous story about the nature and importance of gratitude. On His way to Jerusalem, Jesus traveled along the border between Samaria and Galilee, and as He entered one village, a melancholy group of lepers met Him. They were a mixture of Samaritans and Jews, drawn together by misery. Under normal circumstances, Jews and Samaritans would have nothing to do with each other, but the saying was as true then as it is today: Misery loves company. Take a look at any large group and you're likely to find that the complainers, critics, and cynics cluster together.

Leprosy in those days referred to a number of skin conditions. A leper was always diagnosed by a priest. After an initial examination, a priest could keep a "patient" in quarantine for seven days. If the condition did not improve in that time, he was kept for seven more days. If there still was no improvement, the person was officially declared to be a leper and he was kept in isolation outside the city wall. Food, clothing, and other provisions were brought by relatives and friends and left at a drop-off point—there could be no contact, not even close visual contact, between those who were "clean" and those who were "unclean" with leprosy. The only person a leper could get near was another leper. If by chance a person's skin condition improved, the person might be declared healed but again only by a priest.

The priests were so heavily involved because leprosy was regarded as a manifestation of sin. Anything that rotted away human flesh and led to death was regarded as a curse. In order to keep God's people pure, lepers were cast out of the community.

As Jesus passed through this quarantined place, the lepers stood at a distance and called out to Him, "'Jesus, Master, have pity on us!' When he saw them, he said, 'Go, show yourselves to the priests.' And as they went, they were cleansed" (Luke 17:13–14). Jesus understood their desperation, their feelings of rejection, their anguished spirits. So, without even telling them they were cured, Jesus told them to go and show themselves to the priest so they might get a certificate of cleansing.

I'm not sure that in the modern world we can comprehend the awesome nature of this supernatural mercy. Lepers were looked upon as lower than animals, the scum of the scum. Jesus saw their need and was not repulsed by it—rather, He responded to it with great love and compassion. What Jesus did was far more than mere physical healing. He restored them to society and to jobs, to close conversations with people, to marriage, to entering fully into the worship of the synagogue. He not only gave them back a physical existence, He gave them an opportunity to live a full and rewarding life.

One of the lepers—only one out of ten—came back to Jesus when he saw that he was healed. Even though the man was a Samaritan, he nonetheless threw himself at the Jewish feet of Jesus, where he praised God with a loud voice.

You can almost hear the sadness in Jesus' voice as He asked, "'Were not all ten cleansed? Where are the other nine? Has no one returned to give praise to God except this foreigner?' Then he said to him, 'Rise and go; your faith has made you well'" (Luke 17:17–19).

Nine of the ten took their healing for granted. Nine of the ten took the gift and ignored the Giver. Nine of the ten grabbed what was given to them and thought they owed God nothing, not even a thank-you. Nine of the ten were so caught up in what was happening to them that they gave no thought to God.

Is our society so different? Is the church so different? Think about the current mentality: We have countless people in our society who refuse to work because they think somebody else owes them provision. We have countless adult children who spend their money solely on themselves and expect their parents to provide them room and board. We have countless people in the church who believe it's up to somebody else to give, somebody else to volunteer, somebody else to "perform" on Sundays.

There's an old saying, "He who forgets the language of gratitude can never be on speaking terms with happiness." We wonder at times why we feel misery. I believe the number-one cause is that we have forgotten all the things for which we can be thankful, and we have focused instead on the things we don't have and can't afford. Do even 10 percent of Americans acknowledge God for His provision and His care? In the time of Jesus, only one in ten lepers came back to praise God and to thank Jesus for healing them. There are two great lessons we can learn from the ten lepers.

First, many are our requests, but few are our expressions of thanks.

Take a look at your own prayer life. Compare the percentage of your time before the Lord spent in asking Him for things to the time spent thanking Him for what He has done and praising Him for who He is. Certainly not everybody needs to show gratitude in such a demonstrative way as the one leper who came with a "loud voice" to praise God and who "threw himself at Jesus' feet" to express his thanks. We have no indication, however, that the other nine lepers ever praised God or expressed thanks to Jesus in any way. Even today, we are quick to cry out loudly in need and highly negligent in even whispering our praise.

The story is told of a six-year-old girl riding on a passenger train. She happily roamed the aisle, laughing and playing and making friends with every passenger. It was almost impossible to tell whose child she was. But then the train whistled and roared into a dark tunnel. With a cry of fright, the girl raced back to her seat and threw herself into her mother's arms.

How like that child we are! When the sun is shining, the sky is blue, and the birds are singing, we are full of self-confidence. We don't acknowledge our need to rely on God. But as soon as the shriek of trouble comes and the dark tunnel of problems closes in, we run crying to God. Then, once we are out of the tunnel, we go our merry way again.

How fervently do you voice your praise and thanksgiving to God? Is it with the same fervency that you cry out your requests for His help?

Second, many are the acts of desperation, but few are the acts of gratitude.

People suffering in misery are often so desperate that they will do just about anything to find relief. I heard recently about a man who was diagnosed with cancer. His relatives encouraged him to travel halfway around the world to seek a spiritist healing. Note that I did not say spiritual, but "spiritist." They were recommending that this man go to see a person who believed in false gods and claimed to heal people by the "powers of an angel of light." It is interesting that the term they used for this spirit is the same term the Bible uses to describe Satan (2 Cor. 11:14).

Fortunately, the man suffering from cancer was not that desperate. He said to his relatives, "I'd rather trust Jesus with my death than to trust this spiritist with my life." He made the right decision!

After you have received an answer to your need, a cure for your disease, a solution to your problem, are you as quick to put your gratitude into action as you were to seek a solution to your problem? Do you put as much effort into demonstrating your thanks as you did to searching for restoration?

FOUR QUALITIES OF GRATITUDE

Statistics reveal that only about 20 percent of all church members worldwide give 80 percent of all the tithes and offerings. The same 20 percent also does 80 percent of the volunteer work. There's no way of telling, of course, what percentage of these people give and volunteer with a heart of thanksgiving. But we can be sure of one thing—those who truly are thankful in their praise are also likely to be thankful with their lives. Twenty percent—at most—is a small percentage of thankful people.

How, then, can we gauge our own level of thankfulness? There are four clear characteristics of a thankful person that we can use to measure our own level of gratitude. Gratitude is demonstrated by a determination to express thanks, a promptness in voicing thanks, an intensity in expressing thanks, and a life of humility. Let's look at each of these characteristics.

A determination to express thanks

Those who are truly thankful do not let anything prevent them from expressing their thanks. They do not care what others think or say about their demonstrations of gratitude—they are quick to voice praise and quick to say a heartfelt thank-you.

I pity those who are jaded toward God's generosity in their lives. They seem to believe they have somehow earned God's gifts, or perhaps they don't even recognize God as the source of all good things. They usually are the same people who are never excited about what God is doing in the world. In the end, nothing makes them genuinely thankful.

Promptness in voicing thanks

Those who are truly thankful never hesitate when they are given an opportunity to voice their gratitude. They are quick to join in singing songs of praise, quick to give a word of testimony about the Lord's goodness, quick to give God all the credit for the blessings they enjoy.

A friend told me recently about a phone call he received from a woman who had been healed after a ten-year battle with a brain tumor. He asked her how she was feeling, and for the next fifteen minutes, he told me, he couldn't get a word in edgewise. "She went on and on about all that God had done for her—how He had directed her to the world's best surgeon for her particular type of tumor, how God had ministered to her through the nurses at the hospital, how God had upheld her faith during those ten years, how God had provided for her and her children." He smiled and concluded, "I can't begin to imagine what she might have said if I had asked her to give a testimony about the Lord. I'd probably still be listening to her!"

He was not critical of this woman—but he was amazed. It is so infrequently that we hear a person who is so quick to expound on the goodness and greatness of God.

How many things can you name off the top of your head—quickly—that God has done for you, around you, or in you during the past week? The more we have an attitude of gratitude, the more we will immediately thank God for His blessings as they occur. If you struggle to think of things God has done for you, examine your heart. Are you paying attention to all that He is doing in your life?

Be quick to express your gratitude. Don't wait until testimony time at church. Thank God immediately, on the spot. In fact, take time right now to thank God for His blessing, protection, and provision.

An intensity in expressing thanks

Those who truly are thankful to the Lord have an intensity in their praise. They get excited about what God is doing. They don't thank God with a loud voice so that others will notice them—they are so excited they can't help their loud voice.

Why do we think enthusiasm in giving thanks is so odd? If people scream at the top of their lungs at a ball game, they are considered true fans. But if people scream a loud "Hallelujah" within the walls of the church, they are thought to be fanatics. We have our perception skewed. The most important things to get excited about are the things God is doing in our midst! Be bold in thanking God for all He is doing in your life and in the lives of those you love.

A life of humility

The thankful leper in Luke 17 fell on his face at Jesus' feet. He bowed before Jesus in a supreme act of worship and humility. It was as if he said with all his being, "Jesus, without Your love, Your grace, and Your mercy, I would be nothing. I was dead but still breathing, and You brought me back to life. I was an outcast without hope, and You restored me to my family and to my future."

The grateful leper did not enter into a theological debate with Jesus to try to prove the superiority of his Samaritan beliefs. He did not criticize his fellow Jewish lepers to elevate his own esteem by comparison to them. No—he accepted what Jesus did for him with his whole heart, and he thanked Jesus with his whole heart.

Jesus made an amazing statement to this man: "Rise and go; your faith has made you well." The word *well* really means "whole"—whole not only in body, but in mind, emotions, and spirit. Jesus was not just concerned about this man's physical condition, but about his entire life. Jesus knew the man's deepest need was spiritual, for sin, like leprosy, can cause rejection, loneliness, lack of hope, and fear of the future. This man's humble expression of gratitude before the Lord put him into a position to receive the greater healing in his life—a healing on the inside.

The same is true for us. When we humble ourselves before the Lord in gratitude, a healing work occurs on the inside. When we focus on what the Lord has done for us, we do more than intellectually believe His promises of love and acceptance; we experience firsthand His outstretched arms of welcome, His forgiveness, and His everlasting love. When we fall in humility and gratitude before the Lord in thanksgiving, we open ourselves to the great promise of God in Jeremiah 29:11–14:

> "For I know the plans I have for you," declares the LORD, "plans to prosper you and not to harm you, plans to give you hope and a future. Then you will call on me and come and pray to me, and I will listen to you. You will seek me and find me when you seek me with all your heart. I will be found by you," declares the LORD, "and will bring you back from captivity."

Unless a person has a genuine attitude of gratitude toward God, he cannot grasp all that God desires to do in his future. It is only when we can look back with deep humility and awe for what God has done that we are empowered to believe God for what He will do next in our lives.

THANKSGIVING PRODUCES FAITH AND PEACE

If we are facing a major struggle and need to trust God for victory but find our faith lacking, it's time to examine our life of gratitude. Thankfulness is directly linked to our faith. In fact, thankfulness builds, energizes, and promotes faith. Perhaps that is why the apostle Paul wrote, "In every situation, by prayer and petition, with thanksgiving, present your requests to God" (Phil. 4:6).

If praise is the theme song—the lyrics and melody of our life—then thanksgiving is the rhythm of our heart and attitude. We are to give the Lord thanks in all circumstances (1 Thess. 5:18). Our prayers should always be based upon a foundation of thanksgiving. Paul's instruction to the Colossians was, "Devote yourselves to prayer, being watchful and thankful" (Col. 4:2).

A similar relationship exists between thanksgiving and personal peace. Paul wrote to the Christians at Colosse, "Let the peace of Christ rule in your hearts, since as members of one body you were called to peace. And be thankful" (Col. 3:15). He also wrote, "Do not be anxious about anything, but in every situation, by prayer and petition, with thanksgiving, present your requests to God. And the peace of God, which transcends all understanding, will guard your hearts and your minds in Christ Jesus" (Phil. 4:6–7). In other words, find contentment, and you'll become more thankful. Express your thanks to God and experience peace.

Thanksgiving and peace build on each other. The more we have an attitude of gratitude, the more "settled" we are in our hearts and the greater degree of peace we experience. The more we feel God's peace filling us, the greater our cause for thanksgiving. Thanksgiving puts the emphasis on what God has provided for us, rather than on what the devil has tried to steal from us. The more we see God as our Provider, the greater our trust in Him and the greater the calm that enters our hearts.

Thanksgiving produces greater faith and greater peace in our hearts. And that combination of faith and peace, my friend, is a powerful combination.

CHAPTER 8

PRAISE HONORS GOD
FOR WHO HE IS

P RAISE THE NAME of the Lord!

We read that admonition throughout the psalms, and we hear it frequently in the church today. But what does it mean to praise the name of the Lord?

Shouldn't we concentrate instead on what God does? What is so important about His name?

To answer that question, we need to consider the meaning behind a person's name. Many stories have been told through the centuries about Napoleon Bonaparte, the great French emperor. Some of those stories are jokes, and others are very serious accounts. Most who have studied Napoleon's life believe that he had a good grasp on his place in history.

One story tells of a man who bumped into Napoleon at a party. The man said, "Emperor, I am so pleased to meet you. You and I have the same name." Bonaparte knew this man's reputation for having bad character. He responded with indignation, "You either live up to your name or change it!"

The same could very well be said to us by the Lord: "Christian, live up to your name or change it." We call ourselves followers of Christ and believers in God. We need to live up to our names.

THE IMPORTANCE OF NAMES

In Western culture we don't take names very seriously. But in the Middle East where I grew up, names carry a lot of significance. Parents in the Middle East do not name their children after a movie star or television personality or even based on personal preference. Rather, names are chosen carefully to signify what the parents hope and believe their child will turn out to be. Names are tied to personality, character, abilities, and station in life. In biblical times especially, children were not generally named until the eighth day of their life, which gave the parents a little time to get to know the personality of their baby. Naming a child was, to a significant degree, defining a child.

Today, that process is nearly reversed. Rather than our names defining us, we come to provide a definition for our names. Our character, integrity, and personality are linked to our names so that our names eventually come to mean something as we reach adulthood.

I once heard about a couple who had great difficulty in naming their son. The mother had a fondness for Timothy, which had been the name of her grandfather and an uncle. The father of the boy, however, had grown up with a boy named Timmy who was a real brat—a boy who bullied his peers, was officious with adults, and was forever pulling hurtful pranks. The father wasn't about to name his son Timmy because that name carried such a negative meaning.

We see this link between reputation and name in the business world when people say, "May I mention your name?" as they seek to make a new contact or present a request.

Because names have meaning, it is significant when a name is changed in the Bible, such as the changing of Abram to Abraham, Jacob to Israel, and Cephas to Peter. Every time there is a change of name, a new mission is given to that person—a new identity that relates to a new calling.

But what, you might be wondering, does this have to do with praise? Everything! The names of God, as revealed in Scripture, are not a human invention. They are the way in which God has chosen to reveal His character to us. The names of God are a composite of God's revelation of His nature, His identity, His sovereignty, and His desires. The names tell us who God is; they are an extension of Himself. If you want to know God, get to know His names.

The names of God are evidence that He desires for us to know Him intimately, to praise Him more completely, and to enter more fully into a deep and abiding relationship with Him. There are two names that establish Him as the God Most High, the God of all creation, and as the God who still controls all creation. Let's look at how these two names contribute to a life of praise and devotion to God.

ELOHIM—THE MOST HIGH GOD

The first name that God revealed to humanity was Elohim. That name appears in the Book of Genesis more than 200 times and in the Old Testament as a whole 2,570 times. When the people of God heard the name Elohim, they knew exactly what was meant. The name referred to the "most high" God or the "highest" God—the God above all creation, the God who initiated and created all of life.

To understand the full meaning of this name, we must remember the historical context of the Israelites. In their world, the Canaanites, the Amorites, and all of the other "ites" were worshipping "lower gods"—gods they had fashioned and defined according to human standards. When Abraham proclaimed that there was only one God and that He reigned supreme over the entire universe, he was introducing a radically new concept. At that time, no one else believed in just one God as the originator of all life.

Through the centuries, other cultures clung to their belief in an entire cast of gods related to specific purposes and functions. These gods were limited in power and often in conflict. When the Israelites encountered Canaanites who were worshipping Baal, the god of fertility, the Hebrews responded, "We worship Elohim. He is the One who authorizes the birth of children." When they encountered pagans who were worshipping the god

Shamish, the sun god, giving him homage for his gift of light to the world, the Hebrews responded, "We worship Elohim. He is the One who put the sun in its place and governs its course."

Elohim, the God of all creation, includes all three persons of the Trinity. We know that Jesus was present at creation. As John writes in his Gospel, "In the beginning was the Word, and the Word was with God, and the Word was God. He was with God in the beginning. Through him all things were made; without him nothing was made that has been made. In him was life, and that life was the light of all mankind....The Word became flesh and made his dwelling among us. We have seen his glory, the glory of the one and only Son, who came from the Father, full of grace and truth" (John 1:1–4, 14).

We know also that the Holy Spirit was present as God created the world. In fact, He is mentioned in the second verse of the Bible: "The Spirit of God was hovering over the waters" (Gen. 1:2). God the Holy Spirit has been "moving" and "hovering" over life ever since. He is the Creator of all "newness of life" that we experience in Christ Jesus.

It's important to recognize the Trinity, the full Godhead, because the names of God are not just Old Testament names for the Father. They are names that reveal the nature of the triune God—Father, Son, and Holy Spirit. When we praise the names of God that we find in the Hebrew language, we are praising the name of God in His fullness.

Praise Elohim! He is the one true and living God. He is the only God. He alone is worthy to be worshipped and obeyed. He is our Creator—the Creator of each new day in our life, each new experience we encounter, and each new spiritual work in us. He is the author and finisher of our faith. He is the designer of our life.

El Shaddai—God Almighty

God revealed more of His nature to Abraham, then called Abram, when He revealed another of His names, El Shaddai (Gen. 17:1).

This name literally means "God of Power and Might," or the all-powerful, all-sufficient God. El Shaddai is God Almighty.

The name El Shaddai is a close complement to the name Elohim. If Elohim reveals the God who created and sustains nature, El Shaddai reveals a God who constrains nature, controls nature, and subdues nature. El Shaddai is the God to whom all nature listens and obeys.

Because all things fall under God's rule, God has the power to intervene in the course of nature and change circumstances to conform to His purposes.

Nearly every time God expresses Himself to man as El Shaddai, He indicates that a change will occur in the course of life, and that change will involve a miraculous intervention.

God said to Abram: "I am God Almighty [in Hebrew, El Shaddai]; walk before me faithfully and be blameless. Then I will make my covenant between me and you and will greatly increase your numbers" (Gen. 17:1–2). As soon as God revealed this name, Abram fell facedown before Him. As God continued to speak, He informed Abram that he would have many descendants and that his name would be changed to Abraham, which literally means "father of many nations." God was going to intervene with His power to cause Abraham to father a son, Isaac, even though Abraham's wife Sarai was barren.

God used this same name when He revealed Himself to Jacob, saying, "I am God Almighty [El Shaddai]; be fruitful and increase in number. A nation and a community of nations will come from you, and kings will be among your descendants. The land I gave to Abraham and Isaac I also give to you, and I will give this land to your descendants after you" (Gen. 35:11–12). At the time God spoke these words, Jacob had lost his son Joseph and did not know he was still alive in Egypt. Jacob's other sons were at odds with one another. His sons Simeon and Levi had caused tremendous problems with the powerful and numerous Canaanite and Perizzite tribes that inhabited the land. God was saying to Jacob, in essence, "I am going to intervene on your behalf. You will become a great nation, and you will receive this land that I have promised to you. I am the Lord Almighty—the course of nature and the course of history run according to My will and My plans."

More than three hundred times in the Old Testament, God introduces Himself as El Shaddai. He wants there to be no misunderstanding—He is the ruler and owner of all things. He is the controlling force of all nature and all history.

Because the names of God characterize all three persons of the Trinity, we see aspects of El Shaddai in the life and work of Jesus. One evening after a long day of ministry, Jesus and His disciples entered a small boat to cross the Sea of Galilee. As they sailed, a great storm arose. Owing to the way the winds flow over the mountains into the basin where the sea is located, fierce storms can arise virtually without warning. It's almost as if a giant blender has been turned on high. That night as they sailed, such a tempest arose and their boat began to take on water. They were in danger of capsizing when they finally awoke Jesus, who was calmly asleep at the head of the boat. "Teacher," they cried, "don't you care if we drown?" (Mark 4:38).

Jesus arose, rebuked the wind, and said to the waves, "Quiet! Be still!" (Mark 4:39). The wind died down immediately, and the sea became calm. The disciples were awestruck and said to one another, "Who is this? Even the wind and the waves obey him!" (Mark 4:41).

Who is this? The answer is that Jesus was functioning as El Shaddai—God Almighty, God who governs the winds and the waves and fulfills His plan on the earth.

This incident in the life of Jesus has a close parallel in the Old Testament. In fact, the miracle of Jesus calming the sea is a real-life manifestation of Psalm 107, one of the great redemption psalms that specifically addresses God Almighty's power over humanity and nature. In Psalm 107:23–32 we read:

Some went out on the sea in ships; they were merchants on the mighty waters. They saw the works of the LORD, his wonderful deeds in the deep. For he spoke and stirred up a tempest that lifted high the waves. They mounted up to the heavens and went down to the depths; in their peril their courage melted away. They reeled and staggered like drunkards; they were at their wits' end. Then they cried out to the LORD in their trouble, and he brought them out of their distress. He stilled the storm to a whisper; the waves of the sea were hushed. They were glad when it grew calm, and he guided them to their desired haven. Let them give thanks to the LORD for his unfailing love and his wonderful deeds for mankind. Let them exalt him in the assembly of the people and praise him in the council of the elders.

The psalmist goes on to describe El Shaddai as the one who turns rivers into a desert and fruitful land into salt waste. He also turns deserts into pools of water and parched ground into flowing springs. He sends forth His word and heals and rescues those who cry out to Him from the grave. He leads the humble who are lost in the wastelands to safety and shelter yet causes haughty nobles to wander in a trackless waste. He is God Almighty—nothing is beyond His control.

Do you need God to calm a storm in your life? Do you need healing that He alone can give? Then cry out to El Shaddai. Begin to praise God Almighty! He alone can hold you up when all seems to be crumbling around you. He alone can ride the clouds to summon help for you. He alone can open doors that no one can shut, and He alone can shut doors that nobody can open.

We make a great mistake when we attempt to do things in our own strength. El Shaddai desires to manifest Himself as God Almighty on our behalf. It is time that we begin to see El Shaddai as the prophet Isaiah saw him:

I saw the Lord, high and exalted, seated on a throne; and the train of his robe filled the temple. Above him were seraphim....

And they were calling to one another: "Holy, holy, holy is the
LORD Almighty; the whole earth is full of his glory."

—ISAIAH 6:1–3

Isaiah felt completely undone by what he saw. He cried, "I
am ruined! For I am a man of unclean lips, and I live among
a people of unclean lips, and my eyes have seen the King, the
LORD Almighty" (Isa. 6:5). But then one of the angels flew to
him with a live coal in his hand and touched the prophet's mouth
with it and said, "This has touched your lips; your guilt is taken
away and your sin atoned for" (v. 7). Then the Lord called and
said, "Whom shall I send? And who will go for us?" And Isaiah
responded, "Here am I. Send me!" (v. 8).

When God intervenes on our behalf—when He delivers us,
heals us, restores us, and seems to move heaven and earth on
our behalf—He does so with the purpose of cleansing us and
using us. God not only changes the circumstances around us,
He changes us. He alone is God Almighty who can change the
human heart and give new purpose to a human life.

Praise El Shaddai today! He is at work on your behalf. He is
at work inside your heart. He desires to change you, to change
conditions around you, and ultimately to change the world at
large, in part through the changes He brings about in your life.

THE NATURE OF GOD

We have looked at two of the primary names God used in
Scripture to introduce Himself. Now let's consider His nature in
two areas that relate closely to our praise of Him. One of the
great cries heard in heaven is a cry of praise to God in His roles
of judge and rewarder. The elders who worship God around His
throne in heaven proclaim these words:

The time has come for judging the dead, and for rewarding
your servants the prophets and your people who revere your

name, both great and small—and for destroying those who
destroy the earth.

—REVELATION 11:18

In Revelation 15:3–4 we read that God's judgment is just and
true.

Great and marvelous are your deeds, Lord God Almighty.
Just and true are your ways, King of the nations. Who will
not fear you, Lord, and bring glory to your name?

Let's look at five reasons that we need to praise and honor
God as our judge and rewarder.

God has a right to judge.

The Lord's ways are true; His works are marvelous. He is
absolutely righteous, and therefore, He has the authority to execute justice on the earth. Every nation will ultimately bow to
Him as their King. We find this truth echoed throughout the
Bible:

For we will all stand before God's judgment seat. It is written:
"As surely as I live," says the Lord, "every knee will bow before
me; every tongue will acknowledge God." So then, each of us
will give an account of ourselves to God.

—ROMANS 14:10–12

God alone has the power to judge.

God is the only one with absolute wisdom, absolute righteousness, and absolute power. These are the three things necessary
for a judgment to be eternal. A judge who executes judgments
for all eternity must be without sin or fault, must have a total
understanding of any situation—truly seeing the motivations
of a person's heart as well as the actions of the hand and the
words of his mouth, and must have the ability not only to bring
a person to the bar of justice but to execute the sentence that is

meted out. Only God qualifies to be the judge of all He has created and all that occurs in time and space throughout the ages.

Many people seem reluctant to praise God for His role as eternal and final judge of all people. Perhaps they feel reluctant due to a fear of judgment or because of guilt over past behavior. Let's look at these two obstacles to praising God.

The fear factor

If a person is reluctant to extol God as judge due to fear, he needs to ask himself, "Why am I afraid of God?" There are many reasons a person may be afraid of God—if a person is willfully pursuing sin, he should be afraid!

Rebellion is never ignored by God. It is always subject to God's displeasure. On the other hand, many people have been taught incorrectly about God's nature. They regard Him as being mean-spirited and vengeful. They envision God sitting on a high judgment seat, His eyes piercing the soul of every person with a look of mistrust and suspicion. They believe God sits around waiting for the next person to slip up so He can take pleasure in zapping them with devastating illness, tragedy, or suffering. Nothing could be further from the truth! God is our righteous judge, not one who takes delight in cruel retribution.

The guilt factor

If a person is reluctant to extol God as judge because of guilt, he needs to recognize that guilt comes from unrepented sin. The cure for guilt is to confess sin and receive God's forgiveness for it, and then "go...and leave your life of sin" (John 8:11). We find this great promise of God in 1 John 1:8–9: "If we claim to be without sin, we deceive ourselves and the truth is not in us. If we confess our sins, he is faithful and just and will forgive us our sins and purify us from all unrighteousness" (KJV).

God's judgment is never capricious.

There is no arbitrary enforcement of the rules in God's judgment. When we stand before Him, we will be judged based on what we have done in response to God's commandments. Judgment is based on our obedience, including our obedience in receiving Jesus Christ as our Savior. Take a look at Revelation 16:6: "For they have shed the blood of your holy people and your prophets, and you have given them blood to drink *as they deserve*" (emphasis added).

God's wrath is coming against all who have opposed Him.

God reserves judgment for those who have sought to push Him off the throne so they can reign in His place. Those who seek to destroy God's earth and God's people are subject to being destroyed by God.

Who is it that seeks the destruction of the earth and God's people? Satan. Jesus said very clearly, "The thief comes only to steal and kill and destroy; I have come that they may have life, and have it to the full" (John 10:10). Who are the people who set themselves up to be the enemies of God? There are two main groups. The first consists of people who are in rebellion against God. They know what the Scriptures say, and they know the commandments of God. But they have decided that they are going to live their way rather than God's way. In a second group are those referred to in the letters of Paul as being "apostate." An apostate is a person who knew the gospel and accepted it intellectually or as a social formality but then turned his back on the truth of the gospel. An apostate is a person who denies the Virgin Birth, denies the divinity of the Lord Jesus Christ, denies the Lord's bodily resurrection, denies that Jesus is the only way to heaven, and denies the coming judgment of the Lord.

The Bible provides two great examples of men who betrayed Jesus in different ways. One of them, Judas, followed Jesus, but he always had his own agenda. He followed Jesus because he thought it would be profitable to do so and because he wanted to "use" Jesus to accomplish his own goals. Judas was one of the most privileged of all people in history—he had an opportunity to walk and talk with Jesus on a daily basis. He had an opportunity to hear Jesus' life-changing message firsthand and to witness many of Jesus' miracles. Yet Judas betrayed Jesus to those who sought to crucify Him.

There are those who say Judas was trying to force Jesus into a power play against Rome and thereby instigate a major rebellion among the Jewish population. There are those who say Judas was trying to manipulate Jesus into a display of His supernatural power in order to enlarge the masses that followed Him, in part to increase the amount of financial support that might be provided to Jesus' ministry. They may be right. We'll never know fully why Judas turned his back on Jesus. What we can conclude with certainty is that Judas acted to accomplish his own purposes, and when he failed, he committed suicide. He refused to seek forgiveness from Jesus or surrender his life, including his failure, to Jesus.

But that is not the only outcome possible for those who betray Jesus. Peter also betrayed Jesus by denying three times that he was associated with Jesus. He turned his back on Jesus in Jesus' greatest hour of human need. Peter had boasted of following Jesus to the death, but then within a matter of hours he did not have the courage to admit to a few maidens and common folk that he even knew Jesus.

Like Judas, Peter was guilty of betrayal. But Peter took a very different course after his denial of the Lord. He did not try to hide, ignore, or deny what he had done. Rather, he humbly surrendered all of himself, including his failure, to Jesus. He chose brokenness and confession over arrogance and pride. He became an apostle, whereas Judas became apostate. God's judgment is on the apostate, not the repentant.

God's reward is coming to those who trust and obey Him.

We read in Hebrews that God is a rewarder of those "who earnestly seek him" (Heb. 11:6). God's rewards are going to be given to three groups of people:

1. His prophets—those servants who proclaim
   the truth of God without hesitation, fear, or
   compromise.

2. His saints—those servants who have followed Jesus
   Christ as their Savior and Lord, doing His bidding
   to bring the good news of salvation: a message of
   deliverance to the captives, the illumination of the
   truth to those who are spiritually blind, and wholeness to those who are sick, weak, or hurting.

3. Those servants—both great and small—who fear
   the Lord's name.

God is both our judge and our rewarder, two major aspects
of His divine nature that call for our praise. God has revealed
Himself to us through two of His names: Elohim, the Most
High God over all creation, and El Shaddai, the Almighty God
who remains sovereign over creation. As much as we praise God
for His divine, eternal nature, we also are called to praise God by
the names He uses to reveal Himself.

We turn next to the names that describe God's benevolence to
all who are His children.

CHAPTER 9

PRAISE CALLS GOD BY NAME

O**N SUNDAY MORNING** many churches sing an upbeat praise chorus that calls for believers to honor the Lord with a sacrifice of praise. I can't help but wonder just how many of those who sing this song are able to answer the question "What is a sacrifice of praise?"

We find the answer in Hebrews 13:15: "Through Jesus, therefore, let us continually offer to God a sacrifice of praise—*the fruit of lips that openly profess his name*" (emphasis added). A sacrifice of praise is the confession of the names of the Lord—it is speaking His name in relationship to our personal life.

We must always keep in mind two things as we praise the name of the Lord.

First, our praise is to go to each person of the Holy Trinity. In Revelation 5:13 we read, "To him who sits on the throne and to the Lamb be praise and honor and glory and power, for ever and ever!" God the Father is described in this verse as the One who sits on the throne. God the Son is described as the Lamb.

Second, we must never take our adoption as God's children for granted.

When we truly catch a glimpse of what it means to be God's child, we must hold fast to that truth. We must remind ourselves often that we are heirs and a reflection of our heavenly Father (Gal. 4:6–7). We are in relationship with Elohim, almighty God, and it is a great privilege to say to Him, "Abba"—daddy God.

When we catch a glimpse of all that God has done for us through Christ Jesus, we must hold our new birth as being precious. Because of what Christ purchased for us on the cross, we are members of

His body, we are in relationship with other joint heirs of His grace, and we have a heavenly home that Jesus is preparing for us. We must be ever aware of how privileged we are to be called sons and daughters of the Most High. What a responsibility we bear as we praise God's name!

In chapter 8 we looked at important aspects of God's nature as well as two of His names, Elohim and El Shaddai. In keeping with the sacrifice of praise, lips that confess the Lord's name, let's explore nine additional names that God uses to reveal Himself to us. We will be moved to praise the Lord for the many attributes that are embodied in the names of God.

Yahweh: The God Who Always Is

God's name in English is Jehovah. In Hebrew, the name of God is Yahweh. In the Old Testament, this name for God is used more than any other. In the entire Bible, it is found more than sixty-eight hundred times. The name literally means "to be." It has been translated as "The Ever-Living One" and "The Self-Existing God." Our God depends upon nothing and no one for His existence. He exists in and of Himself. Let us praise our God Jehovah, the Self-Existing God!

Jehovah Jireh: God Our Provider

There are several variations of the name Jehovah in the Old Testament. One of the foremost is Jehovah Jireh. In Genesis 22 God asks Abraham to sacrifice his beloved son Isaac as a burnt offering. At the foot of the mountain, as Abraham and Isaac begin their ascent, Abraham says to the servants who accompanied them on the journey, "Stay here with the donkey while I and the boy go over there. We will worship and then we will come back to you" (Gen. 22:5). Notice that Abraham said "we will come back to you." He had full confidence in God's promises to him—such confidence that he believed if he sacrificed Isaac, God would raise the boy from the dead so the two of them might return together.

On the way up the mountain, Isaac said to his father, "'The

fire and wood are here...but where is the lamb for the burnt offering?' Abraham answered, 'God himself will provide the lamb for the burnt offering, my son'" (Gen. 22:7–8).

After the altar was constructed and the wood laid on it, Abraham bound his son and laid him on the altar. Then, just as Abraham reached to take the knife and slay his son, an angel of the Lord called to him. Abraham replied, "Here I am" (Gen. 22:11). And the angel said, "Do not lay a hand on the boy....Now I know that you fear God, because you have not withheld from me your son, your only son" (Gen. 22:12). Abraham then looked up and saw a ram caught by its horns in a nearby thicket. He went over and took the ram and sacrificed it in place of his son. He called the place Jehovah Jireh, which means "The LORD Will Provide" (Gen. 22:13–14).

The word *jireh* literally means "he sees ahead." God sees what you need before you need it—yes, even before you know you need it. For every task that God gives you, you can be assured that He has already made full provision for all you will need to complete that task. There is no problem for which He has not already prepared a solution. There is no troublesome circumstance or difficulty for which He has not already provided your victory or a way of escape. There is nothing that you face today or in the future that God has not already foreseen and arranged everything you will need.

Praise Jehovah Jireh! God is our Provider today, tomorrow, and for eternity. He knows precisely what we need, and He already has a plan for meeting our needs. Praise our God who sees ahead to provide everything we will ever need!

JEHOVAH RAPHA: GOD OUR HEALER

We read in Exodus 15:26 that God reveals His name as Jehovah Rapha. God makes this promise to His people: "If you listen carefully to the LORD your God and do what is right in his eyes, if you pay attention to his commands and keep all his decrees, I will not bring on you any of the diseases I brought on the Egyptians, for I am the LORD, who heals you."

The word *rapha* means "to heal, to cure, to restore." God does not promise only to heal us in an isolated instance of illness or need. Rather, God says He is healing. His very name is synonymous with healing. He is our wholeness. He is what we ultimately need, no matter what area of weakness or sickness or disease or trouble we encounter.

We see this truth echoed in the New Testament every time Jesus says to a person, "Be made whole." Wholeness is God's desire for us. No disease, nothing that causes us pain or suffering can withstand the healing touch of Jesus. Every knee must bow before the Lord— and that includes anything that opposes God.

Does this mean that God is not true to His name if a person is suffering or if a believer dies from a terminal disease? Not at all. If a Christian is suffering, that person can be assured that God desires to use suffering to bring an even greater reward to that person and to bring an even greater awareness of His presence to others who may witness the person's steadfastness.

All of us are going to die someday, but God tells us that He will never forsake us, not even in death. He is with us always, working all things to our eternal good and bringing us to wholeness. At times God heals areas of our lives so that we experience greater wholeness in this life. In the moment of our death, God seals the wholeness issue completely, and we truly are "made whole" for all eternity.

The apostle Paul was very clear in teaching that God is with us always, whether we live or die. Paul wrote, "If we live, we live for the Lord; and if we die, we die for the Lord. So, whether we live or die, we belong to the Lord" (Rom. 14:8).

What a tremendous encouragement it is to know that God is healing me day by day, week by week, year by year. He is taking all of those broken bits of my life—most of which are completely unknown to me—and mending them with His tender love and great healing power, so that one day I will stand perfectly whole in Christ Jesus before His throne. God does not desire that we live in brokenness. He says to all who turn to Him, "Rise and walk. Be healed. Be made whole." (See John 5:3–9.)

The ongoing work of the Holy Spirit in our world is the work of Jehovah Rapha. It is the Holy Spirit who mends broken hearts, renews degenerate minds, restores shattered relationships, and heals disease. It is the work of the Holy Spirit to conform us to the likeness of the perfect, complete Christ Jesus.

Praise Jehovah Rapha, the God who heals us and makes us whole!

Jehovah Nissi: God Our Banner

In Exodus, God reveals His name to Moses as Jehovah Nissi, which means "the Lord is my banner." What a strange name, you may be thinking. Strange, perhaps, and yet so wonderful!

The Amalekites, a tribe descended from one of the giants who had occupied Canaan, wanted to prevent the Israelites from continuing their journey toward the Promised Land. So Moses called Joshua, the commander of the Israelite army, and said, "Choose some of our men and go out to fight the Amalekites. Tomorrow I will stand on top of the hill with the staff of God in my hands" (Exod. 17:9).

Joshua did as Moses ordered, and Moses, Aaron, and Hur went to the top of the hill. The Bible tells us that "as long as Moses held up his hands, the Israelites were winning, but whenever he lowered his hands, the Amalekites were winning" (Exod. 17:11). To keep things moving in favor of the Israelite army when Moses' hands grew tired, Aaron and Hur took a stone so Moses could sit on it, and then Aaron and Hur held up Moses' hands—one on either side of him—so that his hands remained steady until sunset. That was enough time for Joshua to overcome the Amalekite army.

The "staff of God," which Moses held in his upraised hands, was no ordinary rod. This was the rod that God had given to Moses, the rod that turned into a serpent before Pharaoh and then back into a rod. It was the rod that was thrust into the Red Sea so that the waters parted and the Israelites could walk across on dry ground. It was the rod that Moses had used to strike a rock in the desert so that water gushed forth from it. The staff of God that Moses raised during the battle was synonymous with God's miracle-working power on behalf of the Israelites.

In the aftermath of this great victory the Lord said to Moses, "Write this on a scroll as something to be remembered and make sure that Joshua hears it, because I will completely blot out the name of Amalek from under heaven" (Exod. 17:14). Moses built an altar at that place and called it Jehovah Nissi, the Lord is my Banner, saying, "Because hands were lifted up against the throne of the LORD, the LORD will be at war against the Amalekites from generation to generation" (Exod. 17:16).

As Jehovah Nissi, God raises His miracle-working power over our lives to bring us victory against the enemy of our souls. God provides full assurance that all enemies who seek to destroy His purposes and His people will be defeated.

His staff, or His "banner" over us, is the assurance that we will move forward to achieve all that God has planned and purposed for us.

What are the giants you face today? A giant can be a threat from someone who seeks to destroy you personally or professionally or to destroy your family or business. A giant can be a financial collapse or the nagging fear that failure is around the next bend. A giant can be any form of anxiety that causes a lump in your throat or a feeling of dread in the pit of your stomach. In other words, a giant can be anything that seeks to stop you from proceeding into the fullness of all that God has designated as yours.

I don't know the giants you may be facing, but let me tell you this, giants are nothing when you lift your hands in praise to God and trust Him to be a strong staff of victory over your life. God's ultimate victory is certain—He is far bigger than any giant you may encounter. Not only does He have full power to defeat your enemy and bring you the victory, but He has the power to blot out your enemy so that you will never face that enemy again.

God has the power to completely obliterate the very memory of your enemy so that you are no longer paralyzed by it!

Praise our God, Jehovah Nissi, the banner of victory over our lives today!

Jehovah Mekaddish: God Who Makes Us Holy

The Hebrew word that means holy or sanctified is *mekaddish*. This term is used to describe people who are set apart for divine callings. It is also used to identify the ceremonial utensils that are cleansed and set aside only for use in the temple of the Old Testament. In Leviticus 20:7–8, God says, "Consecrate yourselves and be holy, because I am the LORD your God. Keep my decrees and follow them. I am the LORD, who makes you holy."

Many people are uncomfortable with the word *holy*—they think it refers to unreasonable restrictions on their behavior or appearance. The word *holy*, however, means to be cleansed and separated for God's purposes. All Christians are called to be holy. We are called to be cleansed of our sins by the shed blood of Christ, sealed for God's purposes by the power of the Holy Spirit, and to live righteous lives for God.

Ultimately, it is God Himself who is the Holy Temple in which all of us live and move and have our being. John wrote in his revelation of heaven, "I did not see a temple in the city, because the Lord God Almighty and the Lamb are its temple" (Rev. 21:22).

We are made holy not only by being in God's presence, but also by having His presence in us. The apostle Paul wrote eloquently about our being temples of the Holy Spirit on this earth: "Don't you know that you yourselves are God's temple and that God's Spirit dwells in your midst? If anyone destroys God's temple, God will destroy that person; for God's temple is sacred, and you together are that temple" (1 Cor. 3:16–17).

"Do you not know that your bodies are temples of the Holy

Spirit, who is in you, whom you have received from God? You are not your own; you were bought at a price. Therefore honor God with your bodies" (1 Cor. 6:19–20).

The Holy Spirit who lives within us sanctifies us. If it was up to us to live a holy life on our own strength, or to cleanse our lives by our own efforts, we all would have bombed out long ago. It is not our own efforts but God's work within us that makes us holy. We are holy because He says we are holy.

What a tremendous and awesome mystery that we can be made and called holy by a holy God! Praise God today that He is Jehovah Mekaddish. He is our holiness!

JEHOVAH SHALOM: GOD OUR PEACE

Gideon, the great leader and judge of Israel, made an altar for the Lord and called it Jehovah Shalom, "the Lord is peace." Why was peace so important to him just at that moment?

The Israelites had been living under the tyranny of the Midianites and had no peace. Their enemies routinely invaded their territories to destroy their crops and take or kill their sheep, cattle, and donkeys. The Midianites completely impoverished the Israelites. (See Judges 6:1–6.)

Through the words of a prophet, the Israelites came to realize that they were doing what was right in their own eyes and had forgotten about God. They faced up to the fact that their disobedience was the root cause of their problem. They cried out to God for help, and He responded by sending an angel to speak to Gideon. After the angel had delivered his words, Gideon realized who this visitor really was and he exclaimed, "'Alas, Sovereign LORD! I have seen the angel of the LORD face to face!' But the LORD said to him, 'Peace! Do not be afraid. You are not going to die'" (Judg. 6:22–23).

In response to this visitation from God, Gideon built an altar that he named Jehovah Shalom, which means "the Lord is peace."

Gideon held to the common belief of his day that to see God—to have a direct, face-to-face encounter with the Lord—was to die.

Friend, the truth of God is this: Those who have a face-to-face encounter with God and yield to His will for their lives, bowing before Him in repentance and praise, will be those who live, not only now but forever. It is the person who rejects a personal relationship with God and who refuses to confess that He is the sovereign Lord who puts himself in jeopardy of eternal death.

The only way to experience an abiding, unwavering peace is to know with certainty that God has met us, forgiven us, received us, and has given us the gift of eternal life. Jesus doesn't just give us peace; He is our peace. What He did for us on the cross enables us to enter into a spiritual rest, where there is no longer agitation in our souls caused by guilt, shame, or a fear of eternity.

If you are not experiencing genuine peace—deep, abiding, spiritual peace—then I encourage you to ask yourself, Have I accepted Jesus as my Savior? Do I know with full assurance that I have been forgiven by God and have been received by God as His child forever? Do I have full confidence that I am saved from the consequences of my sin and that this salvation is secure and cannot be taken from me? Do I have full confidence that God has given me the gift of eternal life and that this gift will never be taken from me?

If you cannot answer these questions with a confident and resounding yes, you probably do not have the shalom of God in your heart. And if that is your situation, I invite you to pray right now:

Heavenly Father, I confess to You that I am a sinner and have transgressed Your law. Only You can forgive me for breaking Your commandments. I recognize that breaking Your commandments condemns me to eternal hell. I lack peace of mind because I fear Your wrath.

Thank You for making a provision for my forgiveness through Your Son, who alone kept all the commandments perfectly. He died on the cross as the substitutionary and only complete sacrifice for my sins. I believe that what Jesus did on the cross, He did for me personally. I believe Your Word, which says that Jesus is Your only begotten Son and that my belief in Him grants me life eternal with You. I ask You right now to fill me with Your Holy Spirit so that I might experience Your presence and power at work in my life. I believe You are doing this for me because I believe You always keep Your promises. Amen.

If you have prayed that prayer, or one like it, you have the peace of God.

Shalom, the Hebrew word for *peace,* means far more than an absence of conflict. It refers to far more than contentment or an emotional feeling of being at rest. The word *shalom* means perfect well-being. It means to be filled with a perfect peace, a comprehensive peace, a peace that surpasses our understanding. We will never be free of the enemy of our souls as long as we live on this earth, but we can have peace in knowing that the enemy of our souls has no control over our heart or our eternal future.

Not only will we do battle with the devil throughout our lifetime, but we will continue to experience trouble, difficulties, and pain in our lives. We live in a fallen world, and life is filled with problems. Jesus made this clear when He said, "In this world you will have trouble." But Jesus did not leave His disciples with that negative note. He went on to say, "But take heart! I have overcome the world" (John 16:33).

The common greeting in the early church was "Shalom." Most of the apostle Paul's letters to the churches begin or end with words of grace and peace from God (2 Thess. 3:16). Peace all the time and in every way. How the world longs for that peace! How the Lord longs to give such peace to those who believe in Christ Jesus.

Praise the Lord today that He is our Peace. He gives a calm to our souls that truly is beyond our understanding (Phil. 4:7). He gives a peace that cannot be shaken by life's circumstances. He gives us the peace that all is well with our soul and that we are destined for an eternity in the glorious light of His countenance. Praise Jehovah Shalom!

JEHOVAH ROHI: GOD OUR SHEPHERD

One of the most beautiful images of God in all the Bible is that of a shepherd who leads and cares for His sheep. There is no more tender image to describe the relationship between God and His people. *Rohi* is the Hebrew word for *shepherd*. Perhaps the best-known insight into this name for God is found in Psalm 23:

> The LORD is my shepherd, I lack nothing. He makes me lie down in green pastures, he leads me beside quiet waters, he refreshes my soul. He guides me along the right paths for his name's sake. Even though I walk through the darkest valley, I will fear no evil, for you are with me; your rod and your staff, they comfort me. You prepare a table before me in the presence of my enemies. You anoint my head with oil; my cup overflows. Surely your goodness and love will follow me all the days of my life, and I will dwell in the house of the LORD forever.

The provisions of a shepherd are fully described in this passage. And it's important to connect those provisions with our praise to God our Shepherd:

- Lord, we praise You that You provide for all of our needs so we are not in want. Just as a shepherd leads his sheep to pasture on a daily basis, so You lead us daily.

- Lord, we praise You that You find places of abundant nourishment and rest for us.

- Lord, we praise You that You provide times of spiritual refreshment and retreat for us.

+ Lord, we praise You that You guide us always into right decisions, right beliefs, right attitudes, right words to speak, right actions, right choices so that all of our life brings glory to Your name.

+ Lord, we praise You that You are with us in times of danger and peril and as we face death. You never leave us, and we are grateful.

+ Lord, we praise You that You drive fear from us. We know that in You we have victory over the enemy that seeks to steal from us and destroy us.

+ Lord, we praise You that You have given us Your Word, the Bible, and Your Holy Spirit, to show us the way to live in right fellowship with others—we praise You that You rescue us any time we fall away from the path that is right.

+ Lord, we praise You that You give us Your joy even when we are being persecuted by others.

+ Lord, we praise You that You pour out Your Holy Spirit on us to affirm that we are Yours forever. Lord, we praise You that You have given us Your Son and that His shed blood secures our fellowship with You forever.

+ Lord, we praise You that You are at work always to conform us to the likeness of Christ Jesus and that You desire for us to walk in goodness and love every day of our lives.

+ Lord, we praise You that You have prepared an eternal home for us so that we will never be separated from You.

God's assurance banishes all fears, His provisions make our enemies squirm, and His anointing enables us to do great works in His name. Praise the Lord that He is our Shepherd, Jehovah Rohi!

Jehovah Tsidkenu: God Our Righteousness

In the days of King Josiah, Israel was in dire straits. Judah was heading for a serious fall and the land was oppressed on all sides by violence and crime. King Josiah attempted to bring some reform, but the corruption of society was too entrenched. The spiritual leaders were confused and scattered. The prophets were lying to the people rather than proclaiming God's truth. And then God promised Jeremiah that the day was coming when a righteous king would reign wisely "and do what is just and right in the land" (Jer. 23:5). Jeremiah prophesied, "This is the name by which he will be called: The Lord Our Righteous Savior" (v. 6).

The word *tsidkenu*, Hebrew for righteousness, actually means "up-right, straight, narrow." Today, we might say that righteousness means that a pound is sixteen ounces, not fifteen or seventeen. It means a person's yes means yes, and no means no. It means that we do not deal in deception, we do not waver in our commitment to God's commandments. Even if people hate us for speaking the truth, we speak the truth.

When it comes to the righteousness of God and the commandments of His Word, there are no qualifications for obedience, no justifications for sin. God demands that His people uphold the morality of the Scriptures always and that they live in righteousness before Him.

In 1 Corinthians 1:30 the apostle Paul states that Christ has become our righteousness. By the gift of His indwelling Holy Spirit, Jesus enables us to walk daily in righteousness. The Holy Spirit convicts us of sin so that we know what is right and wrong, and we have the power to say no to temptation and yes to God's will for our lives. The righteousness of God is the root of all integrity. It is the definition of all that is genuinely good in this life.

Praise Jehovah Tsidkenu! Praise God our Righteousness!

Jehovah Shammah: God Who Is Present Always

God is there for you in every moment of every day. God never turns away, never puts us on hold. One of the last statements Jesus made to His disciples was, "Surely I am with you always, to the very end of the age" (Matt. 28:20).

What an awesome truth that, in every moment and every circumstance, all the attributes of God that are embodied in His many names are available to us because He is Jehovah Shammah, always present. This wonderful, awesome God—the Most High God who is our Healer, Victor, and Provider, and who gives us His peace, His holiness, His righteousness, and His power—is with us always. All of God is with us all the time.

Praise Jehovah Shammah! He is the One we can count on immediately and forever.

Praising God by Name Changes Us

I can't help but believe that any time we really begin to praise the many names of God—Father, Son, and Holy Spirit—we will grow in our awareness of His presence with us. The more we catch a glimpse of all that God does and who He is, the more we will want to praise Him. The more we know God through praising Him by name, the more we will feel Him at work in our lives, and the more we will see manifestations of His presence and power all around us.

As I was working on this chapter, I had a one-man revival in my study! As you begin to praise aloud the names of God, I believe that same spirit of revival will flood your soul. You will find yourself energized and renewed spiritually. You will find your attitude growing more hopeful and your faith growing more powerful.

Praise God, the God who reveals Himself to us through His names. When we praise God, let's call Him by name.

CHAPTER 10

PRAISE INVOLVES GENEROUS GIVING

THERE IS NO doubt that blessings follow praise. God responds generously to the praises of His people. We need to understand, however, that blessings are a by-product of our praise. We must never praise God in the hopes of receiving a blessing. The motivation for praise is purely this: we are created to praise the Lord because He is the almighty King of the universe, our Creator, our loving Father, our Savior, our Healer, and our Deliverer.

We must also understand that God is not motivated to bless us because we utter words He likes to hear. Rather, He is motivated to bless us because praise puts us into the right place to receive God's blessing. When we praise Him, we invariably find ourselves convicted of sin. If our hearts are genuine in praise, we will have a heartfelt desire to confess our sin and repent of it. We will seek to change our ways so that our thoughts, words, and deeds line up with God's commandments. As much as praise leads to blessing, it also leads to repentance.

As we move into alignment with God's will and walk daily in obedience before Him, His blessing flows to us. We bless God by our praises, exaltation, honoring, and worship of Him. We also bless Him by our obedience and by pursuing His will for our lives. We bless God by submitting to Him our intellect, emotions, and desires. We bless God by pouring out our love to Him and to others.

Whatever we give fully and freely to God, He multiplies back to us. That is a basic principle of Scripture. Jesus said, "Give, and it will be given to you. A good measure, pressed down, shaken together and running over, will be poured into your lap. For with the measure you use, it will be measured to you" (Luke 6:38).

One of the foremost ways we give to God is to give to those people and ministries that extend God's work on earth. When we give to God as an act of our praise and as an act of obedience, we put ourselves into a great position to receive His blessing.

Now, it's entirely possible to give without praising God. Some people are motivated to give out of guilt. Some people give because their parents instilled this habit during childhood. Some give because they believe it is the right thing to do. Giving can occur without praise, but there cannot be genuine praise without giving. Both the giving spirit and the praising spirit are rooted in an outpouring of the heart.

One of the godly impulses of the renewed heart is to give all of oneself to God, including one's resources. Someone once said that money is "minted personality." Money is the distillation of our time, energy, and labor. Money isn't just something we have— it represents the way we spend our lives. Therefore, when we give money to God's work, we are not just writing a check; we are truly giving part of ourselves back to Him. Our giving is a way of saying, "Lord, I thank You and praise Your name with every part of me. Here is a small part of what You have given me. I acknowledge Your ownership and rule over my life. I acknowledge that You are the source of all things, including my opportunities to work and produce, my harvest of reward, and my well-being. I praise You for all that You have given me. I want to see Your kingdom and Your work on earth extended so that others might also praise You."

WORSHIPPING GOD BY GIVING

I never hesitate to talk about giving because giving is part of our worship of God. And not only does our giving honor God, it also orients our hearts to His work on earth. One of the great men of God, John R. Mott, once said that "giving and soul winning

111

are the Siamese twins of world evangelism."[1] If you are blessed of God, not only will you be a faithful giver, but your love and honor of God will produce a desire to see others won to Christ. If you are going through a harvest time financially, now is the time to praise God even more. Praise Him for the abundance He is pouring out on your life and ask Him what you are to do with the resources He is causing to flow toward you.

At times, however, people who are full of praise experience tough financial situations. I do not deny that. Tough times come to all of us. If you are experiencing a tough time, don't stop praising God and giving faithfully. The windows of heaven will be opened to you again and a blessing of God will be poured out upon you (Luke 6:38). Otherwise God would not be true to His Word. God is faithful in all of life's circumstances, both good and bad. Trust God to turn things around for you.

Our praise honors God, and our giving honors God. The two go hand in hand. However, not everyone approaches giving in the same way. Someone once said there are three kinds of givers: flints, sponges, and honeycombs. This is an interesting concept, because it sheds light on our attitudes toward giving.

The flint-like giver

You may think the flint is a miserly person who doesn't give at all, but that isn't the case. It is possible to get chips and sparks from a flint, but you really have to hammer it.

The story is told of a well-to-do businessman who was visited by a group of Christians asking him to make a large financial gift to their ministry. He responded by saying, "I understand why you are coming to me for this large gift. I am an affluent man who owns a large business. But did you know that my mother is in the most expensive nursing home in this city?"

They said, "No, we didn't know that."

"And did you know that my brother died and left a family of five and that he had very little life insurance?"

"No, we didn't know that either," they said.

"Did you know that my son is deeply religious, and he is giving his life to work among the poor, and his income falls below poverty level?"

"No, we did not know any of this," the spokesman for the group said apologetically.

"Well, then," concluded the businessman, "if I don't give any of them a penny, what makes you think I would give you money?"

That man is a flint. I would conclude that he is as miserly in his praise of God as he is with his money. It would take a lot of hammering—not only by men, but probably also by God—to get a man like that to generously pour out either praise or financial resources. A flint gives only after being hammered and never with thanks or a heart full of praise.

The sponge-like giver

A sponge is a giver who usually has the means to give large gifts, but you really have to put the squeeze on him to get the maximum out of him. Clovis Chapel, one of the great preachers of yesteryear, said, "I love to preach on giving, because I love to see the stingy squirm and the generous rejoice."[2] It is only the stingy who feel the need to squirm, because they hoard what God has given them rather than freely sharing it with others. The generous can rejoice out of a giving heart, but the sponge will give only after being squeezed.

The honeycomb-like giver

The honeycomb is the opposite of both the sponge and the flint. The honeycomb shares freely with others and never needs to be pressured into it. Others know a honeycomb by her generosity and goodness.

The other day I saw a bumper sticker that said, "Tithe if you love Jesus. Any idiot can honk." Honeycomb givers tend to be not only tithers but also generous with their offerings. When they give, they do so out of gratitude to God and with a heart full of praise.

Which kind of giver are you—flint, sponge, or honeycomb?

As you answer that question, think about the kind of praise-giver you are—begrudging or free? Do you praise God only when you feel a preacher or a Bible teacher is hammering you with guilt? Do you praise God only when you feel the squeeze of pressure from others to participate more fully in the praise and worship of God? Or does praise flow sweetly and generously from your life, like honey from a honeycomb?

GENEROSITY HONORS GOD

There are two passages of Scripture that establish a close connection between giving and praise to God. The first is found in the closing chapters of 1 Chronicles; the second, in the New Testament, describes Paul's taking up an offering for the Christians in Jerusalem.

The offering for the temple

In 1 Chronicles 28 we read that David came to the realization that God had not told him to build the temple. David summoned the officials of Israel and said, "I had it in my heart to build a house as a place of rest for the ark of the covenant of the LORD, for the footstool of our God, and I made plans to build it. But God said to me, 'You are not to build a house for my Name, because you are a warrior and have shed blood'" (vv. 2–3).

David then challenged his son Solomon to complete the work. He said, "The LORD has chosen you to build a temple as a sanctuary. Be strong and do the work" (v. 10). David turned over to Solomon all the plans for the temple and its related storerooms and treasuries, as well as the plans for how the service of the Lord was to be conducted and the designations for the weights and types of precious metals that were to be used in making the various utensils of the temple.

Then David made this great statement: "The task is great, because this palatial structure is not for man but for the LORD God. With all my resources I have provided for the temple of my God—gold for the gold work, silver for the silver, bronze for the bronze, iron for the iron and wood for the wood, as well as onyx for the settings, turquoise, stones of various colors, and all kinds of fine stone and marble—all of these in large quantities" (1 Chron. 29:1–2). As the leader of his nation, David made sure that this huge building project would be completed.

But his involvement didn't end with his responsibilities as king of Israel. Notice this statement: "Besides, in my devotion to the temple of my God I now give my personal treasures of gold and silver for the temple of my God, over and above everything I have provided for this holy temple" (v. 3). As king, David had gathered a vast quantity of material for the building of the temple. As an individual follower of God, he also gave his personal wealth. The Bible states that from his personal treasury he provided three thousand talents of gold and seven thousand talents of refined silver. David personally gave 110 tons of gold, worth more than a half billion dollars in today's money. In addition, he gave more than 250 tons of silver. What was David's declared motivation? He saw his gift as a matter of devotion (vv. 3–4).

David's gift triggered a massive outpouring of personal offerings for the temple project. The Bible tells us that "the leaders of families, the officers of the tribes of Israel, the commanders of thousands and commanders of hundreds, and the officials in charge of the king's work" gave great quantities of gold, silver, bronze, and iron, as well as precious stones (vv. 6–8).

This offering was not given by flints or sponges. The people did not have to be hammered or squeezed for a contribution. The Bible declares, "The people rejoiced at the willing response of their leaders, for they had given freely and wholeheartedly to the LORD" (v. 9).

As part of this great day of giving, David praised the Lord in the presence of all who were assembled. He had a profound understanding about the Source of all wealth, declaring of the Lord:

> Everything comes from you, and we have given you only what comes from your hand. We are foreigners and

> strangers in your sight, as were all our ancestors. Our days on earth are like a shadow, without hope. LORD our God, all this abundance that we have provided for building you a temple for your Holy Name comes from your hand, and all of it belongs to you. I know, my God, that you test the heart and are pleased with integrity. All these things I have given willingly and with honest intent. And now I have seen with joy how willingly your people who are here have given to you. LORD, the God of our fathers Abraham, Isaac and Israel, keep these desires and thoughts in the hearts of your people forever, and keep their hearts loyal to you.
>
> —1 CHRONICLES 29:14–18

David then summed up the entire day's proceedings with this command: "Praise the LORD your God" (v. 20). The people responded by immediately praising God, bowing low and falling prostrate before the Lord and their king. The words "Praise the LORD your God" are the last recorded words of King David before he died. What a tremendous testimony they are!

Giving and praise are meant to go together. And when they do, giving is joyful and praise is productive.

The offering for the Jerusalem church

The second passage that powerfully demonstrates the relationship between giving and praise is found in the New Testament. In 2 Corinthians 8, the apostle Paul prepared to return to Jerusalem. He intended to take an offering to the believers there who had been persecuted for their faith and ostracized from the Jewish community, which resulted in extreme financial and material hardship. Paul wrote to the Corinthians, telling them of the plight of the Christians in Jerusalem. He also described the offering he had received from the Macedonian churches:

> In the midst of a very severe trial, their overflowing joy and their extreme poverty welled up in rich generosity. For I testify that they gave as much as they were able, and even beyond their ability. Entirely on their own, they urgently

pleaded with us for the privilege of sharing in this service to the Lord's people. And they exceeded our expectations: They gave themselves first of all to the Lord, and then by the will of God also to us.

—2 CORINTHIANS 8:2–5

Paul then challenged the Corinthian Christians, "See that you also excel in this grace of giving....For you know the grace of our Lord Jesus Christ, that though he was rich, yet for your sake he became poor, so that you through his poverty might become rich" (2 Cor. 8:7, 9).

Note in these verses that Paul applauded the Macedonian believers for their sacrificial giving, noting that they gave "even beyond their ability." Paul also commended the way in which the Macedonian Christians had determined how much to give. They had gone first to the Lord for His counsel, and then they had come to Paul to insist that Paul give them the privilege of sharing in service to the persecuted saints. I don't know a single pastor who would not love to have a group of people come to him and say, "While we were seeking the Lord's will, He told us what to give. Here is our offering. Please use it to bless the believers and extend the gospel to the lost!" What a powerful witness such giving would be, not only to those in the church, but to all who observe the church from afar.

Take note also that the Macedonians were eager and enthusiastic in their giving. They had no feeling that they had lost something or had been diminished in any way. To the contrary. They saw their giving as a great privilege.

The people who gave this offering were, for the most part, slaves or people of meager means. Paul refers to their "extreme poverty." The amount that they gave was certainly not on the scale of the offering given in David's time. But the actual amount is never what is valued by God. Giving from the heart, giving as God commands, giving sacrificially and as an act of devotion, and giving joyfully are the attributes that matter to God.

In both offerings, the one from David's time and the one from Paul's time, the attitude toward giving was the same—an attitude of thanksgiving, willing obedience, and honor to God. The ultimate purpose of both offerings was the same—to meet a practical need and to bring glory to God. The sacrificial nature of the giving was the same. And in both cases, the giving was accompanied by rejoicing and a feeling of personal privilege at being able to give.

Notice as well that the preface to both offerings is the same: dedication to the Lord. David asked the Israelites: "Now, who is willing to consecrate themselves to the LORD today?" (1 Chron. 29:5). Likewise, Paul said of the Macedonians: "They gave themselves first of all to the Lord" (2 Cor. 8:5). Consecration of one's life—deep devotion to the Lord—is the undergirding foundation of genuine praise. It's also the underlying foundation for giving that is blessed by God. It is the very essence of worship—expending one's life and breath in service to God. There is no arm-twisting or pleading in either of these passages. When commitment is present, giving is spontaneous and immediate. When devotion and consecration are present, giving is joyful. In both of these offerings, the money, gold, and precious stones were secondary. The most important facet of their giving was the giving of their hearts.

THE PARTNERSHIP OF GIVING AND PRAISE

When we read these stories of generous giving, we see three themes that are common to both offerings. These same themes extend to our praise of God. First, we acknowledge God's ownership of all things. Next, we regard our giving as a way to extend our ministry and impact. And third, we praise God in our giving.

Giving demonstrates that God owns everything.

If you fail to recognize—not only intellectually but deep in your heart—that God is the owner of all that exists, you have missed the first principle not only of giving but also of knowing

God. God is the source and giver of all things. Ultimately, you and I do not own anything on this earth. Our homes, our cars, our children, everything we have belongs to God. Five hundred years from now, should the Lord delay His return that long, everything in your possession will be gone. There will be no fingerprints of yours left on anything. God, however, will still have everything that currently exists under His control. He will still be in charge of distributing and redistributing all material wealth and tangible goods.

The truth about our possessions is that everything we have is on loan to us from God. He has allowed us to use and to share these things for a season. To have that attitude, we must acknowledge God's ownership of everything.

If a person is a taker, not a giver, or a hoarder and not a sharer, he is likely to think that what he possesses is actually his. He will cling to what he has and feel anger and bitterness against anyone who seeks to use or borrow anything he feels is his. At the core of these feelings of ownership is pride. The person who is a taker and a hoarder is a person who is focused on himself and his "possessions." It is only when we acknowledge that God is the source and owner of all things that we have the freedom to share and to delight in generous giving.

Can you truly say to God from your heart, "All I have is yours"?

Giving extends your ministry and impact.

Giving generously is a way to extend the impact, influence, and ministry of your life. You may feel that you are giving an amount of money, a possession, an hour of time, or an offering of your talent. From God's perspective, however, you are giving something of yourself. God regards your giving as a seed of your entire life.

God established the principle of sowing and reaping at creation, and He repeated it to Noah after the flood: "As long as the earth endures, seedtime and harvest...will never cease" (Gen. 8:22). God takes the seeds that you sow and multiplies them back into a harvest for your life. The more you sow, the greater is the multiplication back to you. Paul stated this clearly: "Whoever sows sparingly will also reap sparingly, and whoever sows generously will also reap generously....And God is able to bless you abundantly, so that in all things at all times, having all that you need, you will abound in every good work" (2 Cor. 9:6, 8).

God's desire for us is abundance—an "abounding" of all things at all times—so that we have not only what we need but an overflow that enables us to grow, give to others, and flourish. However, if we do not give—if we do not sow seed from our life—it is impossible for that seed to be multiplied. Jesus taught this about giving: "For with the measure you use, it will be measured to you" (Luke 6:38).

The opportunity for increase is always present, and it is always God's desire for us. But for us to experience increase, we must open our hearts to God and give of ourselves in the ways He directs us. Paul also said to the Corinthians, "Now he who supplies seed to the sower and bread for food will also supply and increase your store of seed and will enlarge the harvest of your righteousness. You will be enriched in every way so that you can be generous on every occasion" (2 Cor. 9:10–11). Oh, that we might each be "rich in every way" and then "be generous on every occasion"!

Now here's where the rubber meets the road. You can acknowledge all day long that God owns everything. You can believe with all your heart that God will multiply any seed you sow from a consecrated heart. But until you actually give, you are not demonstrating your belief that God is Owner and Source and Controller of all. Until you actually give, you are not planting a seed that God can multiply. You truly confess God's ownership when you give. You confess God's control of your seed when you give.

Neither praise alone, nor giving alone, is enough to put us in position to receive God's blessing. Consecrated praise and devoted giving together are what put us in a position to receive God's amazing, awesome, abounding abundance!

I once thought I could bargain with the Lord on this point. I said, "Lord, You have such a wonderful deal in my being a full-time minister. You really did well for Yourself. You have a man who loves You and praises You and acknowledges that You are the source of all things. You have a man who is willing to work long hours and spend a great deal of energy in service to You."

God replied, "Put in the cash." And, my friend, it was only when I obeyed God fully in my giving and became a regular tither that I began to experience an abundant outpouring of blessing in my life. You cannot say, "Well, I give my ideas at every board meeting. I give my talents whenever I'm asked. I give my time and energy." You also must give your cash. No amount of personal ministry can substitute for giving what has been tangibly given to us by God.

I like the story about the woman who had a palatial home, many servants, and a Rolls-Royce. She had a cook, a gardener, a housekeeper, a secretary, and a chauffeur. Then she died. When she arrived in heaven, she was escorted by Peter to a humble dwelling. She said with disdain, "You mean I am to live in this shack?"

Peter replied, "Well, we can only build with what a person sends up here. You didn't send much."

She was indignant. "Well, what will I drive?"

Peter showed her a rather old, rusted, beat-up vehicle.

"I have to drive this?" she exclaimed. "I'm used to a Rolls-Royce!" Peter just smiled and walked away.

The next day the woman saw her gardener driving a Mercedes and she went back to Peter. "How do you explain the fact that my gardener is driving a better car than I am?" Peter replied, "He sent more proportionately than you did."

The next day, she saw her cook in a nice car. Not long after that, her maid drove by in a really nice car. Every time she saw Peter, she complained. And then one day, Peter saw her happy and singing. Peter asked, "What happened to change your attitude?" She replied, "I just saw my pastor. He was on roller skates!"

God asks not only that we give generously but that we give with joy.

Planting season for a farmer is a joyful season. It's spring—the earth is newly warmed after the winter frost, the buds are popping on the trees, life is being renewed. Planting is a time of great anticipation. That's the spirit God desires for us as we give—not only as we put money into an offering plate, but as we give any gift to Him or to others. He desires for us to give with a feeling of joyful expectancy.

Giving feeds praise, and praise feeds giving.

A tremendous chain reaction is set in motion when we start to praise God and give to God. Our praise encourages others to praise Him. Our giving prompts others to give. We see this cycle carried out in the offering for the temple. David gave and he challenged the leaders to give. The leaders gave and then the people gave, resulting in great rejoicing. (See 1 Chronicles 29:3–9.)

David's gift snowballed into one of the most massive voluntary offerings of all time!

The Macedonian gift had a similar effect. The Macedonians' generous offering for the Christians in Jerusalem prompted the Corinthians to give. Paul wrote of the anticipated outcome of the Corinthians' gift:

> This service that you perform is not only supplying the needs of the Lord's people but is also overflowing in many expressions of thanks to God. Because of the service by which you have proved yourselves, others will praise God for the obedience that accompanies your confession of the gospel of Christ, and for your generosity in sharing with them and with everyone else. And in their prayers for you their hearts will go out to you, because of the surpassing grace God has given you.
> —2 CORINTHIANS 9:12–14

Our giving and our praising are testimonies to others of the work of God. Our giving and our praising call attention to the work of Christ Jesus in the lives of all believers. Our praise and giving produce a hunger for God in the lives of the lost. The most evangelistic thing we can do is to praise God and give simultaneously, and then to couple that with intercessory prayer and words of witness.

There is no limit to what God will do if we will only open our hearts fully to Him, open our lips to praise Him, and open our wallets to give to His work. We each must ask ourselves, "Am I planting numerous and generous seeds of my life? Am I planting all the seed that I can?" Your answer will determine the extent of the blessing you will receive. The person who praises God for who He is and what He has done, and who praises God in tangible expressions of giving and service, is a person who puts himself in prime position to receive the full empowerment and blessings that come from praise.

Those who praise God are automatically put into "receive mode" as the windows of heaven are opened to them. If you are consistently, generously, and genuinely praising God in your life, prepare to receive His blessing. Then use it to extend God's work in this world.

PART IV:

THE POWER OF PRAISE

CHAPTER 11

PRAISE DEFEATS THE ENEMY

P RAISE ACTIVATES GOD'S power in our lives, and nowhere is that more evident than in the realm of spiritual battle. The authentic praise of God empowers us to defeat the devil.

Praise is effective because it involves speaking the truth about God, which has two results. It increases our faith and confidence, and it makes things unbearable for Satan. The devil cannot stand to hear the truth spoken about God. Since his specialty is lies, he cannot abide the truth about God's nature, God's deeds, and God's loving relationship with His people.

Before we use the truth of God against the attacks of Satan, we first need to answer the two most important questions in the Bible. The first is the one Jesus asked His disciples: "What do you think about the Messiah? Whose son is he?" (Matt. 22:42). A person's destiny in eternity hinges on his or her answer.

Jesus made it clear that "if you do not believe that I am he, you will indeed die in your sins" (John 8:24).

The second-most important question we need to answer is found in Psalm 8:4: "What is mankind?" We need to answer this one with God's truth, not man's theory. Is man only a highly developed animal, as Darwin taught? Is man an undeveloped child, as Freud believed? Is man a mere economic factor, as Karl Marx taught?

Plato once defined man as a "featherless bird." Then one of his rivals showed up on his doorstep with a plucked chicken and announced, "Behold! Plato's man." Plato changed his definition of man to "a being in search of meaning."[1] Philosopher

Blaise Pascal had a different view, declaring, "Man is a reed, but a thinking reed."[2] Mark Twain apologized for man by explaining that God made man at the end of the week when He was tired.[3]

King David reflects God's truth in the psalms:

> You have made them [mankind] a little lower than the angels and crowned them with glory and honor. You made them rulers over the works of your hands; you put everything under their feet.
>
> —Psalm 8:5–6

Man cast away his crown of glory and honor when he sinned against God in the Garden of Eden. The God-Man Jesus Christ has returned that honor, dignity, and authority to all men and women who come under the cover of His saving power. Our position today as believers in Christ is once again a position of being crowned with glory and honor.

Why is this important in our ongoing battle with Satan? We find the answer in Psalm 8, which most scholars believe David wrote after he defeated Goliath. This is the testimony of a short, slightly built shepherd who took on a ten-foot heavyweight jousting champion and won. But the battle between David and Goliath has a far deeper meaning than simply a Hebrew shepherd boy conquering the most famous warrior in the Philistine army. The story of David and Goliath is a foreshadowing of the ultimate spiritual battle that was waged a thousand years later between Jesus Christ and Satan. In fact, David's defeat of Goliath is a model for all spiritual warfare in the church today.

Goliath was Satan's champion; David, like Jesus after him, was God's champion. Goliath lost, permanently, due to the mortal wound he suffered. Satan also lost, ultimately, in his showdown with Jesus at the cross. Satan continues to lose as believers take authority over the territory he controls on this earth—including his control of human hearts and minds.

Your proclamation of truth through praise—and especially

your answers to the questions "Who is the Christ?" and "What is man in Christ?"—will make the difference between winning or losing the spiritual battles you face. It is our praise of God that reveals what we believe about the Christ, whose Son He is, and what we believe about man and his relationship to God.

GOD THE VICTOR

Our proclamation of God's truth in praise calls upon the power of the Victor who has already won the battle against Satan. God alone has the power to silence our foe, the avenger (Ps. 8:2). It is no accident that Psalm 8 begins with a proclamation of praise: "LORD, our Lord, how majestic is your name in all the earth!" (v. 1).

David then goes on to describe the "position" of the Lord:

> You have set your glory in the heavens. Through the praise
> of children and infants you have established a stronghold
> against your enemies, to silence the foe and the avenger.
> —PSALM 8:1–2

Remember that David most likely wrote these words after defeating the giant Goliath. This Philistine soldier was a great foe whose fierceness was multiplied because he was fighting a "vengeance" battle to pay the Israelite army back for its previous victories over a small Philistine army. We see this same dynamic at work today. If you chart the course of conflict in the Middle East, a great deal of it has to do with "vengeance" battles—the old eye-for-an-eye mindset that is still at work between enemies. Goliath did not seek the death of all Israelites. No, he wanted to put all of Israel in subjection. The winner of this battle would have the right to force into slavery all the people of the losing nation. Enslavement would grant power and authority to the victor and would bring pain and suffering, a tearing apart of families, and a loss of worship traditions to the losing side.

Satan is waging a similar vengeance battle today. He lost the spiritual war at Calvary, and he's been wreaking vengeance on believers ever since. He doesn't want to kill you right away. First, he wants to force you into slavery, to do his bidding, to heed his commands. He wants to enslave your body with addictions and excesses, your mind with heresies and paralyzing doubts, your spirit with guilt and shame. Satan wants to inflict pain and physical suffering, take away your joy, rip apart your family, and utterly destroy your relationship with Christ Jesus and His church.

Goliath mocked and taunted the Israelites, saying, "This day I defy the armies of Israel! Give me a man and let us fight each other" (1 Sam. 17:10). Satan mocks and taunts us today, crying out to the depths of our spirit, "I defy your faith! Come out and fight me, and let's see who wins." Will we stand up in indignation and righteousness, as David did, and say, "Who is this uncircumcised Philistine that he should defy the armies of the living God?" (1 Sam. 17:26). Or will we cower in fear, just as King Saul and the rest of the Israelite army did?

It's time for us to call upon the powers of heaven and humble ourselves before God, crying out, "LORD, our Lord, how majestic is your name in all the earth!" (Ps. 8:1). It's time we see God as the Victor over all His enemies and over all those who seek to take vengeance on His people. When you are faced with a spiritual struggle—discouragement or temptation, fear or doubt—the best course of action is to exalt the position of God as the great Victor in the battle for the souls of men and women. To win the battle against Satan's vengeance, you must praise God for sending Jesus to win the eternal war for your soul. Praise God for resurrecting Jesus on the third day so that you have the hope of eternal life. Praise Him that you heard the gospel, and that He convicted you of your sinful nature by the power of His Holy Spirit so that you desired to receive Jesus as your Savior. Then praise God for securing once and for all the redemption of all who believe in Jesus Christ. Praise God that He loves you enough to lead you daily so you might be conformed to the image of Christ.

You can spend hours praising God for your salvation, and you will not even have scratched the surface of how much God is worthy to be praised. In the midst of spiritual warfare, praise God that Satan is our defeated foe forever and ever. Praise God that we will live in the light of His glory for all eternity. God secured our salvation through Christ, and that is our power against Satan's attacks.

God's Limitless Love

The more we praise God for who He is, the more awesome He becomes in our understanding. Then we must ask the questions "Why should this holy, perfect, all-powerful, all-wise God care about me? Why should He care about *any* human being?"

David asked the question about man's relationship to God this way: "What is mankind that you are mindful of them, human beings that you care for them?" (Ps. 8:4). If you don't answer that question in light of God's Word, the devil will ask you a question along these lines: "Who do you think *you* are? Why on earth would God want to save *you*? Just look at you! Why would God want *anything* to do with you?"

David doesn't offer an explanation for God's love. He simply offers the truth of our God-created position:

> You have made them [mankind] a little lower than the angels and crowned them with glory and honor. You made them rulers over the works of your hands; you put everything under their feet: all flocks and herds, and the animals of the wild, the birds in the sky, and the fish in the sea, all that swim the paths of the seas.
>
> —Psalm 8:5–8

My friend, there is no explanation for why God desires to be in relationship with you other than His unconditional love for you. There isn't anything you have done to warrant His love. It truly is a free and undeserved gift from God.

So many people engage in countless good works to try to earn enough points to win God's love. They strive to earn His affection, His attention, and His salvation. And all the while, they don't realize that they *already* have His love and His attention. They have the promise of His salvation held out to them with the open arms of Jesus on the cross.

As long as we live on this earth, none of us will ever know why God loves us. But the truth stands nonetheless. God loves us. And out of His great love for us, He crowned us with glory and honor (Ps. 8:5). He made us ruler over all the works of our hands, and He put all the other creatures of the earth under our authority.

What motivated Jesus to come to earth to die an agonizing death so that you might be saved? Love. What motivated Jesus to die in your place so that you might be spared the eternal consequences of your unforgiven sin? Love. What motivated Jesus to send the Holy Spirit to seal your belief in Him? There is only one answer: love.

Everything that Jesus was, and all that He did, is a reflection of God's love in terms that we can understand. Jesus hugged little children, tenderly dealt with those who confessed their sins, healed the sick, gave hope to the downtrodden, delivered those oppressed and possessed by demons, and set free those who were trapped by shame and guilt. Jesus said, "Anyone who has seen me has seen the Father" (John 14:9). The disciples who followed Jesus knew He was motivated by love.

Read what the apostle John wrote:

> Everyone who loves has been born of God and knows God. Whoever does not love does not know God, because God is love. This is how God showed his love among us: He sent his one and only Son into the world that we might live through him. This is love: not that we loved God, but that he loved us and sent his Son as an atoning sacrifice for our sins.
>
> —1 JOHN 4:7–10

There is no explanation for God's unconditional love. Neither is there any satisfactory explanation for the mercy, forgiveness, and grace that flow from that love. Nevertheless, God loves us without limit.

Praise God for His infinite, unconditional, everlasting love! Praise God for the mercy and forgiveness that flow to all sinners who accept the sacrifice of His Son. Praise God for the grace that flows to you to enable you to live a godly life in an ungodly world. But don't stop there. Praise God that His love for you will never falter and will never cease!

God's Purpose for Us

God lovingly made man with the capability to rule the works of His hands and to put into subjection all of the other creatures God had made (Ps. 8:6–8; Gen. 1:28). His command to us has never changed: "Be fruitful and increase in number; fill the earth and subdue it. Rule over the fish in the sea and the birds in the sky and over every living creature that moves on the ground" (Gen. 1:28).

We hear this same theme echoed in the words of Jesus as He issues a final command to His disciples: "All authority in heaven and on earth has been given to me. Therefore go and make disciples of all nations, baptizing them in the name of the Father and of the Son and of the Holy Spirit, and teaching them to obey everything I have commanded you. And surely I am with you always, to the very end of the age" (Matt. 28:18–20).

We are created by God with authority to accomplish His purposes on this earth. We have not only the natural authority God gave to all humans at creation but the spiritual authority given to us at our spiritual rebirth. God has commissioned us to fight the battles that He has already won on our behalf. We are to bring to the earth the tangible victories that Christ Jesus has already won for us in the spiritual realm!

Praise God that He has created you with a crown of glory and honor (Ps. 8:5). Praise God that He has created you with a purpose and has authorized work for you to do, souls for you to win, and spiritual strongholds for you to take as you intercede in prayer. Praise God that He has given you a measure of authority to establish His plan and further His kingdom on earth.

If we truly catch a glimpse of God as our great Victor over everything the devil throws at us, we will respond in praise. If we truly catch a glimpse of God's great love for us and the awesome plan God has for our lives, there is only one thing we can say in response: "Lord, our Lord, how majestic is your name in all the earth!" (Ps. 8:9).

Psalm 8 ends just as it begins, with praise for God's exalted position over all things. We are moved to praise God for the great love that motivated Him to be mindful of us and to care for us. We praise God for our salvation. So, we end where we began: God is worthy to be exalted over all things.

Arming Yourself for Battle

David faced Goliath with praise on his lips and a slingshot in his hand. His praise may have startled Goliath, even put him off guard. But praise alone did not cause Goliath to fall. David still had to pick up the stones and load his slingshot. He still had to run at Goliath. He still had to swing that slingshot and let loose a stone that sailed toward Goliath at the speed of a bullet fired from a Colt .45.

What, then, are we to do today that will back up our praise with "spiritual muscle"? First, we are to arm our praise with Scripture. When Jesus faced Satan in the wilderness, He mentioned nothing that was based on His human thoughts or feelings. Rather, He quoted Scripture. The devil said, "Tell these stones to become bread" (Matt. 4:3). Jesus responded, "Man shall not live on bread alone, but on every word that comes from the mouth of God" (Matt. 4:4; Deut. 8:3).

The devil said, "Throw yourself down [from the highest point of the temple]" (Matt. 4:6). Jesus replied, "Do not put the Lord your God to the test" (Matt. 4:7; see also Deuteronomy 6:16).

The devil said, "[All the kingdoms of the world] I will give you... if you will bow down and worship me" (Matt. 4:9). Jesus said, "Away from me, Satan! For it is written: 'Worship the Lord your God, and serve him only'" (Matt. 4:10; see also Deuteronomy 6:13).

The apostle Paul, in writing to the Ephesians, told them to put on the whole armor of God in their spiritual battles. He taught them to stand their ground with the defensive armaments of a belt of truth, a breastplate of righteousness, a shield of faith, a helmet of salvation, and their feet shod with readiness that comes from the gospel of peace. But what was the offensive weapon that Paul specified? "The sword of the Spirit, which is the word of God" (Eph. 6:17).

Jesus quoted Scripture in response to the devil's temptations. Paul taught believers to arm themselves with the Word of God. We must use this same weapon in our spiritual warfare today.

Gather your stones.

If you are facing a particular battle right now, go to God's Word and gather your stones. David chose five smooth stones for ammunition. I recommend that you find at least five verses of Scripture that directly address the area that Satan is trying to attack. Study carefully what God's Word is saying, and get the whole of God's wisdom on the issue. Be convinced within your spirit that God is the Victor over the situation you are facing and that He desires to work on your behalf for your eternal good.

Load your slingshot.

Next, write down the verses that directly address the difficulty you are facing. Read those verses aloud again and again every day for as long as your difficulty lasts. Let the truth from God's Word sink deep into your spirit. Memorize and quote those verses as you go about your daily tasks.

Take aim and fire.

Any time you feel fear rising up in you, any time you feel threatened by the enemy of your soul, any time you find yourself doubting God's goodness or His victory, that's the time to start praising God. Praise Him for being the author of an unfailing and unchanging Word. Praise Him for what He has said to you in Scripture.

+ "Father, I praise You for Your Word to me in John 15. You are the Vine, I am a branch. Your words are abiding in me and I will be fruitful. You said that if I remain in You, I can ask whatever I wish and it will be given to me. I want to remain in You always. Here is what I ask You to do: Defeat the enemy on my behalf. Drive the devil far from me. Protect me and flow through me. Let my life be fruitful for You."

+ "Father, I praise You that You are always trust-worthy. According to Your Word in Psalm 25, You are the One who lifts up my soul. I trust in You right now, O God. Your Word says that You will do certain things for the man who fears the Lord; You will instruct him in the way chosen for him. You will cause him to spend his days in prosperity. You will make Your covenant known to him and reveal insights into Your own nature. My eyes are on You, Lord. I declare that You are the Victor in my life and that You will defeat the doubts and confusion that the devil is throwing at me. You will defeat the devil as he tries to steal from me. You will turn my poverty to prosperity."

+ "Father, I praise You right now for Your Word in Psalm 28 that tells me You always hear my cries for mercy. You are my strength and my shield. My heart trusts in You. I declare that You are the

Victor over the enemies who seek to do evil to
me and who show no regard for the works of the
Lord. I declare right now that You are the Victor
over those who tear down. I praise You for hearing
my cries and for carrying me like a Good Shepherd
through this trial."

At times, your praise may need to turn into a recitation of verses.
Let your singing give way to "slinging" Scripture at your enemy:

+ "Whoever dwells in the shelter of the Most High will
rest in the shadow of the Almighty" (Ps. 91:1).

+ "Rise up, Judge of the earth; pay back to the proud
what they deserve" (Ps. 94:2).

+ "My help comes from the Lord, the Maker of heaven
and earth. He will not let [my] foot slip—he who
watches over [me] will not slumber" (Ps. 121:2–3).

+ "Those who trust in the Lord are like Mount Zion,
which cannot be shaken but endures forever. As
the mountains surround Jerusalem, so the Lord
surrounds his people both now and forevermore"
(Ps. 125:1–2).

+ "The scepter of the wicked will not remain over the
land allotted to the righteous" (Ps. 125:3).

+ "But you, Lord, are a shield around me, my glory, the
One who lifts my head high" (Ps. 3:3).

When you take aim at the devil with Holy Scripture, he either
flees or falls. Either way, you experience God's peace and God's
sovereign provision. Jesus called the devil the father of all lies, so
he never stays around when the truth of God is being spoken. He
runs as far away as possible from the truth. The truth of God's
Word pummels the devil when it is couched in a spirit of praise

and thanksgiving. Praise based on the Word of God defuses the power of Satan. The praise of God renders the devil mute.

PRAISE AND DAILY INTERCESSION

When we grab hold of the fact that God is the majestic, sovereign ruler over all things, and therefore, the supreme Victor over all forces of evil, we begin to count it all joy that God puts us into position to engage in spiritual warfare. The key to winning spiritual battles is praise.

Why is praise essential to spiritual victory? Get this fact clear: Nothing neutral ever comes out of your mouth. When you say, "This is going to be a bad day," you are predicting the quality of your day. When you say to your child, "You will never amount to anything," you are cursing your child's future.

The way we conquer Satan and the way we establish the goodness of God on this earth is the very reverse of these examples. When you say, "This is the day the Lord has made," you are establishing the tenor of your day with faith in the Lord as the victor over all things. When you say, "What a great time to be alive in the Lord Jesus!" you are inviting the Holy Spirit, the Lord and Giver of Life, to rule the circumstances in which you find yourself. When you say to your child, "Praise God—He has given you wonderful tasks to do to bring Him glory and to win souls for His kingdom," you are establishing an eternally rewarding destiny for your child.

In our praise we defeat the forces of hell that seek to destroy us, undermine our faith, diminish our influence, and demolish our integrity. When David went running down the mountain to meet Goliath in the Valley of Elah, he shouted:

> You come against me with sword and spear and javelin, but I come against you in the name of the LORD Almighty, the God of the armies of Israel, whom you have defied. This day the LORD will deliver you into my hands, and I'll strike you down and cut off your head. This very day I will give the carcasses

of the Philistine army to the birds and the wild animals, and
the whole world will know that there is a God in Israel. All
those gathered here will know that it is not by sword or spear
that the LORD saves; for the battle is the LORD's, and he will
give all of you into our hands.

—1 SAM. 17:45–47

What a phenomenal shout of praise! Goliath had shouted personal insults at David. David shouted praise to God at Goliath.
Likewise, when the devil comes at you insulting you about who
you are not, what you don't have, and what you will never be,
immediately shout back praise to God for giving you a purpose,
an inheritance, and everlasting salvation! When the devil comes
to give you the long list of reasons that you aren't worthy of God's
goodness, shout back praise to God for His unsurpassed love that
has been poured out on you. When the devil comes at you to tell
you that you are going to lose big-time, shout back praises to God
for being the victor of your life for all time!

Jesus quoted Psalm 8 when the Pharisees rebuked Him during
His triumphant entry into Jerusalem. He said, "From the lips
of children and infants you, Lord, have called forth your praise"
(Matt. 21:16). What did He mean? What did the psalmist mean
when he first sang those words? Think for a moment about the
faith of a young child. A child doesn't have doubts about God. A
child doesn't have reasons that God should or shouldn't do certain things. A child simply loves and believes and hopes. And so
must we.

In the end, the great strength of our praise in warfare is the
fact that our praise declares that God loves us and that God has
gained the victory over Satan and that's that. God loves and God
wins. Period.

Truly the name of our Lord is majestic in all the earth!

CHAPTER 12

PRAISE OVERCOMES NEGATIVE CIRCUMSTANCES

M ANY YEARS AGO a major soft drink company had an advertising slogan: "Things go better with..." I'm not sure what "things" the slogan referred to, but let me assure you that *all of life* goes better with praise.

You may be thinking, "Sure, things go better in the spiritual and emotional realms when we praise God. But does praise bring about any meaningful changes in my daily life in the physical realm?"

Yes, indeed! Praise changes our physical circumstances in two ways, as we see in Psalm 67:

> May the peoples praise you, God; may all the peoples praise you. The land yields its harvest; God, our God, blesses us. May God bless us still, so that all the ends of the earth will fear him.
>
> —PSALM 67:5–7

The first change that is produced by praise is God's blessing on whatever our desired harvest may be (v. 6). Second, there is an impact on the lives of those who see God's blessing in our lives. When others see God blessing us, they are prompted to fear the Lord (v. 7). This means, for one thing, they will be less likely to attack us openly. They still might attack us secretly, but at that point our praise gives way to the spiritual warfare of prayer and faith. As we use the weapons of God in spiritual warfare, our enemies in the spiritual realm are defeated. That is when real changes can happen. Victories we would never have thought possible become reality in the physical world.

When we read the Scriptures, we see two dramatic examples of this truth. The first is the story of Jehoshaphat, king of Judah, and the amazing military victory that God brought to pass. The second is the miraculous experience of Paul and Silas when they were freed from prison in Philippi.

PRAISE BRINGS A MILITARY VICTORY

Jehoshaphat, one of Judah's righteous rulers, did his best to turn the Israelites back to God. But when he appointed Levites, priests, and heads of families to administer the law of the Lord, major trouble erupted. Problems often come our way just when we are doing the most to return to obedience.

Three groups of people mounted a vast army and attacked Judah with the goal of capturing Jerusalem. Alarmed at the news of the advancing army, Jehoshaphat did the two wisest things any person can do. First, he "resolved to inquire of the LORD," and then he "proclaimed a fast for all Judah" (2 Chron. 20:3). When we are faced with opposition or potential danger, we need to run to the Lord to see what lesson He wants us to learn and what course of action He wants us to take. And then we need to fast and pray until we receive His answer, asking the believers around us also to fast and pray.

Jehoshaphat went to the temple, where he began his prayer with praise: "LORD, the God of our ancestors, are you not the God who is in heaven? You rule over all the kingdoms of the nations. Power and might are in your hand, and no one can withstand you" (v. 6). He then asked God to defend His people, acknowledging that "we have no power to face this vast army that is attacking us. We do not know what to do, but our eyes are upon you" (v. 12). The king surrendered everything to God. He claimed no power or wisdom on his own. He completely submitted his ego and his crown to the Lord.

God answered Jehoshaphat with very specific instructions, delivered through prophetic words given to a man named Jahaziel:

"Do not be afraid or discouraged because of this vast army. For the battle is not yours, but God's. Tomorrow march down against them. They will be climbing up by the Pass of Ziz, and you will find them at the end of the gorge in the Desert of Jeruel. You will not have to fight this battle. Take up your positions; stand firm and see the deliverance the LORD will give you, Judah and Jerusalem. Do not be afraid; do not be discouraged. Go out to face them tomorrow, and the LORD will be with you" (vv. 15–17).

Jehoshaphat bowed down with his face to the ground in worship before the Lord at these instructions, as did all the people of Judah who had gathered with him. Then the Levites stood and praised the Lord "with a very loud voice" (v. 19).

And look how the battle was waged! Early the next morning, Jehoshaphat said to the people, "Have faith in the LORD your God and you will be upheld; have faith in his prophets and you will be successful" (v. 20). He then appointed men to sing to the Lord and to praise Him "for the splendor of his holiness" (v. 21). He put them at the head of the army, where they led the way toward the battle praising and singing, "Give thanks to the LORD, for his love endures forever" (v. 21).

As they began to sing and praise, the Lord set ambushes against the Ammonite, Moabite, and Meunite armies. These armies turned on one another and destroyed one another, so that by the time the men of Judah looked out over the desert, they saw only dead bodies. Not a single enemy soldier had escaped. So rather than wage a battle, Jehoshaphat and his men gathered the plunder. It took them three days to gather up the wealth, and even then, they had to leave some things behind.

On the fourth day, they all assembled in the Valley of Beracah to praise the Lord (v. 26). They returned with joy to Jerusalem, and once in the city, they went immediately to the temple with harps, lutes, and trumpets to praise God.

This tale of military victory is a praise story from beginning to end. God's people experienced a great blessing, and in the end, the "fear of God came upon all the kingdoms of the countries when they heard how the Lord had fought against the enemies of Israel. And the kingdom of Jehoshaphat was at peace, for his God had given him rest on every side" (vv. 29–30). Not only was Jehoshaphat and his nation blessed, but the surrounding nations developed a fear of God and His might.

If you are facing persecution or an attack in any area of your life, begin to praise the Lord. God may not direct you with detailed instructions as He directed Jehoshaphat. But then again, He may. What we can know with certainty is this: It is right to praise God at all times and in all places, in times of peace and in times of struggle and opposition. In fact, we need to praise God *especially* in times of difficulty, pain, and opposition.

Praise Opens Prison Doors

In the New Testament we read a story with many similar elements. Paul and Silas enjoyed a productive ministry in Philippi. However, as they were walking with other believers to "the place of prayer," they were trailed by a slave girl possessed by a spirit that enabled her to recognize spirits and predict the future. This young woman would walk along shouting: "These men are servants of the Most High God, who are telling you the way to be saved" (Acts 16:17). She kept this up for many days.

The evil spirit was not speaking through her to promote the cause of Christ but rather to try to shut down the ministry of Paul and Silas. Finally, Paul became so angry at the evil spirit that he turned to the girl and commanded the spirit, "In the name of Jesus Christ I command you to come out of her!" (v. 18). Instantly the spirit departed.

The owners of the slave girl were upset, of course, because they realized that her value as a fortune-teller was gone. They stood to lose a great deal of income because of Paul's action. So, they seized Paul and Silas, dragged them into court, and accused them of throwing the entire city into an uproar by advocating customs that were unlawful for Romans to practice. That was an exaggeration, but they were able to whip up a frenzy of opposition, and the magistrates ordered Paul and Silas to be stripped and beaten (vv. 20–22).

Battered and bruised—physically wounded by the flogging and abused by the false accusations—Paul and Silas were then ushered to a prison cell. The jailer was ordered to watch them closely, so he put them in the inner cell and fastened their feet in stocks. What had started as a walk to a place of prayer ended in confinement in a pitch-black cell in chains, pain, and, no doubt, bloody gashes and bruises from the flogging they had received.

What was their response? The Bible tells us that "about midnight Paul and Silas were praying and singing hymns to God, and the other prisoners were listening to them" (v. 25). Paul and Silas were not moaning in pain or complaining about their false imprisonment, but rather praising God at the top of their voices. They turned imprisonment into an opportunity for evangelism, singing loudly to bring the gospel and encouragement to the other prisoners.

They transformed a jail sentence into a praise service.

And suddenly, as they were praising and praying, "there was such a violent earthquake that the foundations of the prison were shaken. At once all the prison doors flew open, and everybody's chains came loose" (v. 26). The jailer awoke, and when he saw the prison doors standing open, he assumed all the inmates had escaped, which would have meant not only his job but also that his own life would be in jeopardy. He drew his sword and was about to kill himself when Paul shouted, "Don't harm yourself! We are all here!" (v. 28).

The jailer called for lights, rushed in, and fell trembling before Paul and Silas. He brought them out of their cell and said, "'Sirs, what must I do to be saved?' They replied, 'Believe in the Lord Jesus, and you will be saved—you and your household'"

(vv. 30–31). They preached the gospel to the jailer and to all the others from his house, and the jailer and his family were baptized.

Not only had God freed Paul and Silas from the chains of their imprisonment, but when morning broke, the magistrates sent word to the jailer, "Release those men." The magistrates too had experienced a change of heart overnight. The jailer released Paul and Silas with a blessing (vv. 35–36).

Simply being released from jail wasn't enough for Paul, however. He demanded that the magistrates escort them out of prison since they had been beaten publicly without a trial, even though they were Roman citizens. The magistrates were alarmed and immediately came to appease them and escort them from prison. They asked Paul and Silas to leave the city, which they did—but not before they met with the believers to encourage them and share the news of this great victory that the Lord had won (vv. 37–40).

When other believers see us praising God in the midst of opposition or suffering—and they see how God brings us through difficult times—their faith is strengthened. Others around us who are suffering are encouraged. And those who aren't believers very often desire to accept Jesus as their Savior.

Praise Empowers Us to Stand Firm

In the year 1900 the city of Galveston, Texas, was swept by a tidal wave that caused a great loss of life and destruction of property. Soon after, a prominent engineer was hired to design a sea wall that would withstand any future storm. The engineer was told that cost was not a factor—the safety of the city was all that mattered. He undertook the challenge, and four years later the sea wall was complete. It consisted of a massive barricade five miles long, and it rose seventeen feet above the high-tide mark. The engineer, who considered this sea wall to be his crowning achievement, proudly declared that not even the fiercest gale could destroy the wall and threaten the city of Galveston.

Years later this engineer was working on a project in Alaska when he received a telegram saying that a tidal wave had again swept over Galveston and had demolished the massive sea wall he had designed. Turning to his associates, the engineer said, "This is impossible. I built it to stand. There must be some mistake." He had the utmost confidence that the telegram was in error.

He was right. The telegram had been sent in panic before anyone had thoroughly surveyed the damage or the wall. Even today, the sea wall that protects the city of Galveston stands as firm as the Rock of Gibraltar.

My friend, God wants to build you so that no tragedy or trial of life can overwhelm you and cause you to fall. He desires to build you up so that as the storms of life blow around you, you will stand firm and declare, "God is my hiding place."

What brings us to the place where we know without any doubt that the accusations the devil roars against us are nothing but empty lies? What brings us to the place where we know without any doubt that all persecutions against us will ultimately end in failure and that God will receive all glory for our deliverance? What builds us up to the place where we can demonstrate our faith in action—interceding with powerful prayer, speaking and acting in bold confidence of our salvation, doing the mighty works of God in the midst of an unbelieving and spiritually lost world?

The only answer is faith that is born of praise. Praise gives us the enduring power—the persevering, refuse-to-give-in-to-the-devil power—to withstand the enemy until we see the victory that we know with certainty is God's will for us. In the face of calamity, we must express the praise of the psalmist:

> I will extol the LORD at all times; his praise will always be on my lips. I will glory in the LORD; let the afflicted hear and rejoice. Glorify the LORD with me; let us exalt his name together. I sought the LORD, and he answered me; he delivered me from all my fears. Those who look to him are radiant; their faces are never covered with shame. This

poor man called, and the LORD heard him; he saved him out of all his troubles. The angel of the LORD encamps around those who fear him, and he delivers them. Taste and see that the LORD is good; blessed is the one who takes refuge in him. Fear the LORD, you his holy people, for those who fear him lack nothing.

—PSALM 34:1–9

Regardless of how dire your circumstances appear, you can live in faith that God is sovereign over the universe. Nothing happens without His permission. So live in the confidence that He protects you and provides for you. Don't ever doubt that God's everlasting arms are underneath you. His wings are sheltering you. His eyes are watching over you. His powerful hand is upholding you.

God's Spirit is empowering you. His mighty army is sent to defend you. God is with you. Yes, He is ever-present with you.

CHAPTER 13

PRAISE EMPOWERS PRAYER AND MINISTRY

R. A. TORREY, A great man of God in decades past, once said, "Prayer is the key that unlocks all the storehouses of God's infinite grace and power....All that God is and all that God has is at the disposal of the one who prays."[1] If I were to add to that statement, I'd say, "Praise supplies the power to turn the key of prayer in the storehouse lock!"

Praise opens us up so that we can pray with greater faith and greater effectiveness. Praise reflects our acknowledgment of all that God is and all that God has done, is doing, and has promised to do. Praise sets the stage for prayer that is focused, specific, and powerful.

Jesus Himself established the priority of praise in our prayers. In the model prayer that He gave to His disciples, He taught them to pray, "Our Father in heaven, hallowed be your name, your kingdom come, your will be done, on earth as it is in heaven" (Matt. 6:9–10). Jesus was teaching those closest to Him that praise is the beginning of prayer.[2]

When we hallow the name of God, we "make holy" His name. We reverence and praise God's nature and His presence with us. When we seek God's kingdom to come to this earth, we are praising all that God has done, is doing, and has promised to do in the future to conform our lives and the entire world to His plan and purpose.

It is only *after* we have praised God for who He is and what He does that we are to bring our requests before God. After praising the Lord, we ask Him for our daily bread, for forgiveness, for deliverance from times of testing, and for deliverance from the evil one (Matt. 6:11–13).

Jesus also made it clear that praise is the finale to prayer. After we have made our requests known to God, Jesus taught that we should close our prayers by saying, "For thine is the kingdom, and the power, and the glory, for ever" (Matt. 6:13, KJV). Prayer begins *and* ends with praise.

When we close our prayers with praise, we are asking God to edit our requests and to answer our petitions in His timing, according to His methods, and in ways that perfectly fit His will. We are yielding all authority to God, including authority over the way in which our prayers are answered. We are yielding all methodology to God, including the details of when and where and through whom He may choose to provide for us, protect us, or reveal Himself to us. We are yielding all honor to God, giving Him credit for any good work that is accomplished on our behalf, accomplished through us, or accomplished in us.

The bulk of the Lord's Prayer, the prayer that Jesus gave to His disciples as a model, is praise. The prayer begins with praise, and petitions flow from it. Then the petitions lead us back to praise.

We see this same pattern in many of the apostle Paul's letters. Time and again, he opens his letters with words of thanksgiving and praise. To the Ephesians, he began his letter by saying, "Praise be to the God and Father of our Lord Jesus Christ, who has blessed us in the heavenly realms with every spiritual blessing in Christ" (Eph. 1:3). To the Corinthians, he wrote, "Praise be to the God and Father of our Lord Jesus Christ, the Father of compassion and the God of all comfort, who comforts us in all our troubles, so that we can comfort those in any trouble with the comfort we ourselves receive from God" (2 Cor. 1:3–4). We see a similar pattern of praise and thanksgiving at the beginning of his letters to the Philippians, the Colossians, and the Thessalonians. Paul was a man of praise and gratitude, and he wanted those he taught to adopt the same attitude.

Praise Empowers Our Prayer

How does praise relate to our petitions in prayer? The more we praise God, the more we realize not only that He knows about our needs, but that He desires to meet our needs. God wants us to ask Him to provide for our needs not so that He will become better informed about them, but so that in asking we will become more aware of what is truly nagging at our hearts, burdening us, or challenging us. Praise puts us in a position to receive answers from God. Consider the person who praises God:

"You are all-powerful, Father. You can do all things."

"You are all-merciful to Your children, Father. You desire to bless us in all ways."

"You are patient and forgiving, Father. You long to draw all Your children close to You."

"You are the Victor over the enemy in every situation and circumstance, Father. You have already won the battle against the devil."

After giving God such praise, what petition could we make that God isn't already supremely concerned about and fully capable of handling?

A woman once told me about an experience she had in a worship service during a retreat. The minister asked people to focus on the cross in the room and simply to adore the Lord. Adoration may be considered "silent praise." It is the focusing of our mind toward thanksgiving and praise.

The woman found herself silently praising God for His many attributes and the things He had done for her. And then she said, "I felt as if the Lord had come to occupy the empty place next to me. His presence was so profound, I felt certain that if I opened my eyes He would be sitting right there. I began to think, 'What should I say to Him?' I mulled over my prayer list and thought, 'Perhaps I should ask the Lord not for things in my life but for the things I desire Him to do in the lives of friends and relatives who are sick or struggling.' Then, almost immediately, I thought, 'But He already knows all about any situation I would bring up.'

"I concluded there's only one thing to say to the Lord. I will tell Him I love Him. 'I love You' was the only thing that felt right. But I also knew that when I said those words to Him, He would only smile. He already knew that I loved Him. Even so, I knew He would enjoy hearing it again."

That incident changed this woman's prayer life. "After that experience," she said, "I realized that praise is really the heart of prayer. It puts all prayer requests in the right perspective. It keeps the focus on God as the One I am trusting always with every detail, every challenge, and every relationship of my life."

Does this mean we should not voice our petitions to God? Not at all. Praise, however, causes us to focus on the things that truly are significant and truly are part of God's will. God invites us to make our needs and desires known, but ultimately prayer is not a means to obtain everything we want. Instead, it is a process of laying hold of God's will for our lives. Our prayers are answered in the affirmative when they line up with God's plan and purpose for us.

But how can we know if the things we have requested are within His will?

We begin by considering all the things that are promised to us in God's Word. At times, those promises are directed only to certain individuals, so we must be certain that we are claiming promises that God makes to *all* believers. Consider some of the things the apostle Paul wrote to the early church regarding his petitions for them:

+ To the Ephesians, Paul wrote: "I keep asking that the God of our Lord Jesus Christ, the glorious Father, may give you the Spirit of wisdom and revelation, so that you may know him better. I pray that the eyes of your heart may be enlightened in order that you may know the hope to which he has called you, the riches of his glorious inheritance in his holy people, and his incomparably great power for us who believe" (Eph. 1:17–19).

+ Paul told the Thessalonians: "We constantly pray for you, that our God may make you worthy of his calling, and that by his power he may bring to fruition your every desire for goodness and your every deed prompted by faith. We pray this so that the name of our Lord Jesus may be glorified in you, and you in him, according to the grace of our God and the Lord Jesus Christ" (2 Thess. 1:11–12).

You may have noticed Paul's focus on spiritual matters. Does that mean we shouldn't ask the Lord to meet a specific financial need or heal a specific ailment? Not at all. However, we do need to make our petitions in light of the truly important things—those things that count for eternity. Remember what Jesus said to His disciples:

> Do not worry about your life, what you will eat or drink; or about your body, what you will wear. Is not life more than food, and the body more than clothes? Look at the birds of the air; they do not sow or reap or store away in barns, and yet your heavenly Father feeds them. Are you not much more valuable than they?…
>
> And why do you worry about clothes? See how the flowers of the field grow. They do not labor or spin. Yet I tell you that not even Solomon in all his splendor was dressed like one of these. If that is how God clothes the grass of the field, which is here today and tomorrow is thrown into the fire, will he not much more clothe you—you of little faith?
> —MATTHEW 6:25–26, 28–30

Jesus concluded,

> But seek first his kingdom and his righteousness, and all
> these things will be given to you as well.
>
> —MATTHEW 6:33

Our prayers must always focus on God's eternal plan and His divine purposes. Certainly the Lord desires to meet our practical needs, and we are not condemned by God when we voice those needs. We grow in faith and develop spiritual maturity, however, when we redirect our petitions to those things that truly bring a person to spiritual wholeness and deliverance from all evil.

Praise leads us into God's intimate presence, and once we are there, we discover His will for us. Praise leads us to the place where we receive power from God to stand steadfast against Satan's temptations, oppressions, and assaults.

PRAISE ENERGIZES OUR FAITH

Praise empowers our prayers and also builds up our faith so that when we make our petitions before God, we pray with expectancy and confidence that we will receive God's best. Consider the person who praises God, saying: "You are mighty, O Lord. You have made heaven and earth. You are the Author and Finisher of all faith, the Creator and Sustainer of all that is good. You are almighty God."

How can a person who praises the Lord in that way then pray a weak, insipid "God, I hope You will meet my need" prayer? Our praise builds up our faith, putting us in a position to pray, "*All* things are possible for my God." That was the stance of the apostle Paul when he wrote from a prison cell, "I can do all this through him who gives me strength" and "my God will meet all your needs according to the riches of his glory in Christ Jesus" (Phil. 4:13, 19).

Time and again we find in the Scriptures the admonition to pray "with faith":

+ "If any of you lacks wisdom [or any other trait that God desires for you to develop], you should ask

God, who gives generously to all without finding
fault, and it will be given to you. But when you
ask, you must believe and not doubt, because the
one who doubts is like a wave of the sea, blown
and tossed by the wind. That person should not
expect to receive anything from the Lord. Such a
person is double-minded and unstable in all they
do" (Jas. 1:5–8).

+ Jesus said, "If you believe, you will receive whatever
you ask for in prayer" (Matt. 21:22).

+ Jesus also said, "Whoever believes in me will do
the works I have been doing, and they will do even
greater things than these, because I am going to the
Father. And I will do whatever you ask in my name,
so that the Father may be glorified in the Son. You
may ask me for anything in my name, and I will do
it" (John 14:12–14).

It is those who pray with faith who see God break the strongholds of the enemy. It takes faith to declare that you are God's
property and the devil is a trespasser. It takes faith to confess that
your body is the temple of the Holy Spirit who lives in you and
works through you. It takes faith to stand against the enemy of
your mind and body.

Deep in the Arabian desert, a small fortress stands silently on
the vast expanse of ageless sand. The fortress was used often by
Thomas Edward Lawrence, better known as Lawrence of Arabia.
Though unpretentious, the fortress provided great security to
those inside it. Old-time desert dwellers talked about how confident Lawrence became regarding the fortress. He trusted that it
would help him withstand any assault from his enemies.

Let me assure you that the name and shed blood of Jesus Christ
provide a fortress for us that is far stronger than any stone walls
erected in the Arabian desert. The assault against us is spiritual;

our weapons of praise and prayer are also spiritual. When our faith is founded on the goodness and power of our mighty, incomparable, and unconquerable Savior and Lord, our faith is *strong*.

Praise puts us into the position of seeing God as bigger and more powerful than any enemy coming against us. Praise puts us into the position of truly believing that "the one who is in you is greater than the one who is in the world" (1 John 4:4). Praise builds our faith so that we make our petitions with boldness and confidence. As we read in Hebrews, "Therefore, brothers and sisters, since we have confidence to enter the Most Holy Place by the blood of Jesus…and since we have a great priest over the house of God, let us draw near to God with a sincere heart and with the full assurance that faith brings.…Let us hold unswervingly to the hope we profess, for he who promised is faithful" (10:19, 21–23).

Praise gives us confidence in the Lord. Peter and John were arrested for healing a lame man at the Beautiful Gate of the temple. After the authorities threatened them never to preach about Jesus again—something they flatly refused to agree to—John and Peter returned to a group of believers and reported all that had happened. Rather than cower in fear, these believers began to raise their voices in praise and prayer, saying:

> Sovereign Lord…you made the heavens and the earth and the sea, and everything in them. You spoke by the Holy Spirit through the mouth of your servant, our father David: "Why do the nations rage and the peoples plot in vain? The kings of the earth rise up and the rulers band together against the Lord and against his anointed one." Indeed Herod and Pontius Pilate met together with the Gentiles and the people of Israel in this city to conspire against your holy servant Jesus, whom you anointed. They did what your power and will had decided beforehand should happen. Now, Lord, consider their threats and enable your servants to speak your word with great boldness. Stretch

out your hand to heal and perform signs and wonders through the name of your holy servant Jesus.

—Acts 4:24–30

The Bible tells us that after the believers prayed, "the place where they were meeting was shaken. And they were all filled with the Holy Spirit and spoke the word of God boldly" (Acts 4:31). These believers from that day on began to demonstrate the power of God in word and deed.

Are you under attack? Are you feeling defeated? Are you tempted to compromise or give up? Then there is only one thing to do: sing praises to the Lord! Your praises will lead you to pray bold prayers. And when you do, God will respond by empowering you with His Holy Spirit so you are strengthened to demonstrate the power of God. Praise leads to faith, which leads to boldness in prayer, which leads to an outpouring of God's Spirit, which leads to confidence and boldness in action. Praise becomes our solid footing in the face of evil, establishing our hearts so that we cannot be tossed about by ill winds.

Praise Emboldens Our Ministry

The ultimate expression of praise to God is found in the way we live our lives. A life that is obedient to the Lord—to His written commandments and to the daily guidance of the Holy Spirit—is a life of praise. And the person who is empowered by the Holy Spirit to live boldly and confidently—taking every opportunity to speak the name of Jesus and to demonstrate the love of God—is a person who is motivated toward service at every turn in the road. Abundant praise leads to effective, merciful witnessing to the lost. Abundant praise leads to consistent, love-laden ministry to the needy.

How can I make such claims? Because when we faithfully exalt the goodness and forgiveness and provision and protection of God, we realize that we are the recipients of these blessings. When we realize that we are the recipients of God's tender care, we develop a growing desire to give tender care to others and to lead them to God so they will also receive His blessings.

When we focus on all that God is, we desire to become more like Him. We are motivated to extend ourselves to others. When we focus on all that God has done for us, we desire to do good for others. We are motivated to give of ourselves to others. When we focus on how wonderful it is to be called a child of God and we recognize the awesome reality that we have been saved from the devil's clutches and an everlasting hell, we are driven to lead others to Christ so they too might be saved.

Throughout the Old Testament, the worship of God was framed in terms of ritual and service in the tabernacle and then later in the temple. To worship God was to "serve" God in His temple. It was to do those things that were pleasing to God—to offer the sacrifices of praise that He desired, to make the sacrificial gifts He commanded, to engage in righteous living, to meet the needs of widows and orphans and others in need. Worship was an outward action, not simply words that were spoken.

So too is our worship today. God is looking for those who are not only hearers and speakers of His Word but also doers of His Word (Jas. 1:22). When we walk away from a time of praise, we are to put our praise into action—using our hands and feet to show others that we truly believe what we have said about God.

We declare to Jesus in our praise: "You are God incarnate. You are our Savior. You died to pay in full the debt for our sin. You are the only way to a relationship with God. You are the Lord." When we walk away from praising Jesus in that way, our next two challenges are these: to say those same things to someone who doesn't know Jesus as his Savior or who is discouraged in his faith walk, and second, to live in such a way that we express in our behavior the reality that Jesus is God incarnate. He is the Savior. We have been forgiven of our sins. We are in right relationship with God. We are following Jesus as our Lord.

What we believe about Jesus becomes what we praise Jesus for. What we believe Jesus is and has done becomes our witness to others. What we say to others about Jesus becomes the pattern for the way we will live out our lives before them. Praise not only empowers our prayer and energizes our faith, it also emboldens our ministry to others. It makes us effective in living out what we believe about God. Praise the Lord for the gift of praise!

Living in the Power of Praise

As we move into a life of praise, we soon discover that praise builds on itself. The more we praise God, the more desire we have to praise Him even more.

As we praise the Lord, we develop a growing awareness of God's nature, power, and majesty. If we are intentional about the praises we are voicing, we cannot help but become awestruck by God's sovereignty, holiness, and power. The more we praise the Lord, the more reasons we find to praise Him. The more we praise the Lord, the greater our desire to praise Him. The more we praise the Lord, the greater delight we find in praising Him. The more we encounter the providence, grace, and glory of God, the more we will find ourselves wanting to praise Him again.

Start praising God today, and I guarantee you'll never be the same again. Start praising God today, and you'll never want to stop!

LIVING IN THE POWER
OF PRAISE

WE PRAISE GOD because He alone is worthy of glory and honor, not because we want to receive His blessing. But it is clear that praising God changes our life. It increases our faith, opens our eyes to God's nature and His work on earth, supplies power to resist the attacks of Satan, changes adverse circumstances, and makes us more effective in ministering to others. Growing in praise is an adventure—an empowering adventure.

This study is designed to guide you on a life-changing experience of praising God. The questions in each lesson will help prompt reflection and action that will change your approach to praise. Keep your Bible open as you do this study, and ask the Lord how to best apply these truths.

This book and study guide can be used for both individual and group study. The questions for each chapter are divided into three parts. The first section is called Reflecting on Praise, with questions designed to trigger personal reflection, meditation, prayer, and sometimes action. These questions are also useful for small-group discussion.

The second group of questions is called Practicing Praise. In many cases, you will be challenged to write out a statement or to make a list that will help you apply the truth contained in that chapter. I encourage you to buy a notebook that you can use as your praise journal. Write out the suggested lists and statements in it, and refer to your journal often in your times of praise and prayer.

The third group of questions is called Small Group Options. These activities are specifically designed for use in a group study. Use these suggestions to prompt discussion, sharing, prayer support, and shared experiences of praise. (If you use this study in a group setting, make sure each group member reads the related chapter in the book before the group discussion.)

CHAPTER 1

PRAISE BRINGS GOD NEAR

B EFORE ANSWERING THE study questions, read the book's introduction and chapter 1, which look at some of the blessings that come to us through praising God. As you read the chapter, think about times in your life when God has seemed distant.

REFLECTING ON PRAISE

1. Ask yourself three questions about the way you practice praise:

   + What do you truly believe about God's nature? Are you convinced that He is the only One who truly deserves your praise and adoration?

   + Do you believe that God is completely good in His actions toward you?

   + Do you have questions related to God's love for you, His desire to bless you, or His ability to work all things for good in your life? If so, make a list of those questions in your praise journal and set aside time to pray over them after you have been praising God.

2. Are you satisfied with the level of praise in your life? If not, in what areas do you feel you are neglecting the praise of God?

3. Are you satisfied with the rate of your spiritual growth? How could increasing your praise of God lead to increased spiritual growth and greater maturity in the Lord?

PRACTICING PRAISE

1. Spend fifteen minutes every morning during the next week doing nothing but praising the Lord (no prayer requests allowed). At the end of seven days, evaluate the effect that praising God has had on your life, your daily challenges, and your love for God. Specifically, note:

   + What changes can you identify in your feelings and attitudes?

   + Did you find yourself less angry or frustrated, especially when faced with negative circumstances? (If not, give this exercise another week. Commit to fifteen minutes of pure praise every morning.)

2. Think about how you would like God to work in your life. Identify one key area, such as your health, a relationship, finances, or productivity at work, and then commit to the following:

   + Find five verses or passages of Scripture that relate directly to God's sovereignty over that area of your life. Write down these verses. Next to each verse, write out a statement of praise to God. Begin to praise God, aloud, for His promises to you, for His power at work in your life, and for His provision for every need that you face.

   + Identify specific situations related to your area of concern. For example, an appointment you need to make or a conversation you need to have. Before you address that situation, praise God aloud for who He is, for His love and guidance, and for His blessing in your life and in the lives of others.

SMALL GROUP OPTIONS

1. Invite group members to bring their praise journals with them to your next meeting.

2. Ask each group member to be prepared to share a blessing, an insight into God's character, or a positive benefit associated with his or her regular expressions of praise to God.

CHAPTER 2

PRAISE CONNECTS US
TO HEAVEN

I N CHAPTER 2 the author shows how praise connects us with the heavenly realm. As you read the chapter, think about the joys of heaven and the praise of God that is offered continually in heaven.

REFLECTING ON PRAISE

1. Read Matthew 6:19–21 and Matthew 12:33–35. Our words reveal what we truly treasure in our heart. Think about the things you talked about the most in the past two days. What does your conversation reveal about the things you treasure most? Do you find yourself valuing the things of heaven or the things of earth?

2. Reflect on this statement from chapter 2: "There is no mention [in Revelation] of individuals offering praise alone in heaven. The praise in heaven is corporate, and it is praise that is joined to the praise of all others who exalt God and proclaim Jesus as Lord." How can you begin praising God regularly together with your spouse, your children, a close friend, or other members of your study group?

3. What is the prevailing atmosphere of your life? What can you do differently, starting today, to make praise the atmosphere of your life—to make your words, thoughts, and attitudes more positive, more God honoring, and more filled with praise?

PRACTICING PRAISE

1. In heaven the angels and the saints continually praise God. Because praise connects us with God's realm, we can join our praises with those being spoken right now in heaven. Use the words of heavenly praise found in Revelation 4:8–11; 5:9–14; and 7:9–12 in your own prayers of praise today.

2. Throughout this week use the verses from Revelation to inspire your own words of praise to God.

SMALL GROUP OPTIONS

1. If group members brought their praise journals, invite them to share a meaningful insight into praise from the past week.

2. End your meeting with each group member sharing a blessing that he or she has experienced as a result of praising God.

3. Plan now to begin your next meeting by joining together in a time of spoken praise to God.

CHAPTER 3

PRAISE DEMANDS PERSONAL CHANGE

A S YOU PREPARE for this study, consider some of the ways praise challenges you, as discussed in chapter 3. As you read the chapter, think about personal changes God wants to make in your life.

REFLECTING ON PRAISE

1. Conduct a personal praise inventory by asking yourself:

   + How often do words of praise spring from my lips?

   + How much passion do I put into my praise to God?

   + How long do I praise God before I run out of things to praise Him for?

   + What attributes of God are most frequently mentioned in my praise?

   Reflect on your answers. Ask God to reveal ways in which you need to expand your praise life.

2. Think about your beliefs related to God the Father, God the Son, and God the Holy Spirit. Ask yourself:

   + What do I believe about God's nature?

   + What do I believe He desires to do for me?

   + From what has He delivered me?

+ In what ways is God blessing me today?

3. Consider the value that you place on your relationship with God. Is there anything that you value more than this saving relationship? If so, make a list of these things in your praise journal. Then reflect on God's love that was demonstrated in the sacrifice of His Son to save you from your sins.

4. Look back over questions 1–3. Make a list of the things that might be preventing you from praising God more than you do. Set aside time to pray over those deterrents to praise, asking God to help you make praising Him the highest priority.

PRACTICING PRAISE

1. Identify one area in which God wants you to change. Think about your attitude, energy level, relationships, spiritual perceptions and sensitivity, and desires. Write out a statement of praise to God for:

   + His desire to change you for the better

   + His ability to change your life

   + His loving methods for bringing about change in your life

Carry these praise statements with you and read them aloud—voicing your praise to God—several times a day for the next week.

2. Write the following thoughts on note cards and post them where you will notice them regularly during the day:

   + Praise God more often.

   + Praise God longer.

   + Praise God with greater passion.

After two weeks ask yourself, "Am I actually praising God more often, for longer periods of time, and with greater intensity?" If not, why not?

3. If you succeed in increasing, prolonging, and intensifying your times of praise, think about the changes you see as a result. Consider especially your attitude, your energy level, your relationships, your spiritual perceptions and sensitivity, and your desires.

SMALL GROUP OPTIONS

1. Begin your meeting by joining together in a time of spoken praise to God.

2. If group members brought their praise journals, invite each one to share a blessing or a struggle related to his or her praise life during the past week.

3. Before the meeting ends, share with one other group member an ongoing challenge you are facing in your life of praise. Ask that person to pray for you this week.

4. At the next meeting check with the person who asked you to pray for him or her to see if the person has experienced any changes.

CHAPTER 4

PRAISE TOUCHES DEEP EMOTIONS

MANY OF US avoid things that touch our deepest emotions. However, God calls us to honor and praise Him with all of our being, including our emotions. As you read chapter 4, think about any reluctance you might have about praising God with your emotions.

REFLECTING ON PRAISE

1. Reflect on this statement from chapter 4: "[God] is worthy of all expressions of our love, including our expressions of deep emotion." How easy is it for you to freely express your emotions? What would help you become more comfortable in expressing emotion to those closest to you, to friends at church, and to God?

2. Read 1 Chronicles 15:27–28 and 2 Samuel 6:14–15. If you had been part of the parade of Hebrews bringing the ark of the covenant to Jerusalem, how would you have felt when you saw others singing and dancing before the Lord? Would you have joined in? Why or why not?

3. How is God speaking to you about expressing your emotions when you praise Him?

PRACTICING PRAISE

1. Tomorrow, while you're driving to work or running errands, play some worship/praise music. Sing along with this musical

expression of praise to God. If the song is an upbeat one, clap while you're stopped in traffic.

2. As you are walking, jogging, or working at your computer this week, play praise choruses over your headphones. Silently praise God along with the words to the praise songs.

SMALL GROUP OPTIONS

1. Make a joyful noise to the Lord as a group! Play some worship/praise music and sing together. Make sure group members feel the freedom to stand, sit, or kneel and to clap their hands during this time of praise. If anyone in your group plays a musical instrument, invite that person to play along.

2. If someone asked you to pray for him or her at your last meeting, be sure to check with that person for an update.

3. Ask group members to bring their praise journals to your next meeting so you can extol God together. (See the study for chapter 5.)

CHAPTER 5

PRAISE CALLS US TO BEAR WITNESS

MOST CHRISTIANS DON'T connect praising God with witnessing to those who are outside God's family. However, Scripture makes a clear connection between honoring God and sharing the gospel. As you read chapter 5, look for ideas on ways you can combine your praise with opportunities to talk to others about God.

REFLECTING ON PRAISE

1. The author defines extolling God as proclaiming His goodness and greatness in the presence of others. Are you ever reluctant to extol God when others are around? Reflect on why that may be so.

2. What do you believe God will do in your life in the next twelve months? For each thing you want God to do, identify two passages of Scripture that verify this as a work He desires to do in your life and in the lives of all His children.

PRACTICING PRAISE

1. The author defines adoration as a personal expression of worship to God. Spend some quiet time today simply adoring Jesus as your Savior.

2. Introduce God and His care for us into at least three conversations during the coming week. Purposefully extol Him to others, even if it is just to say, "Praise the Lord," when you hear good

news. Or when a friend tells you about a struggle, say, "I believe God is going to help you with that problem; He's greater than any problem on this earth."

3. Make up your own praise song—the words don't need to rhyme; the tune doesn't need to be one anybody else can sing or remember. Voice your praise to God this week in song.

4. In your praise journal, write down a description of how God has revealed Himself in your life. Use personal terms, such as "my Savior," "my Lord," and "my Healer." List as many descriptive terms as you can.

SMALL GROUP OPTIONS

1. If group members brought their praise journals, invite each person to share a personal description of God.

2. At the end of your meeting, build up one another's faith by praising God together for being our Savior, our Lord, our Healer, our Shepherd, and other personal descriptions that have been shared by group members.

CHAPTER 6

PRAISE WARS AGAINST OUR PRIDE

PERHAPS THE BIGGEST obstacle to praise is our unwillingness to let go of pride. Praise honors God for who He is, which puts us in a position of submission to Him. As you read chapter 6, think about ways your pride limits your praise.

REFLECTING ON PRAISE

1. The author maintains that praise and pride cannot coexist, since one will crowd out the other. Praise shifts our focus away from self and fixes our gaze on God. Praise calls for our full surrender to God and His will. Have you fully surrendered every area of your life to the Lord? How did you feel when you fully surrendered everything to Him? (If you have not done this, why not do it today?)

2. Reflect on your own struggle with pride. In what ways are you asking God to help you lay down your selfish desires so you can pursue His desires, plans, and goals for your life?

3. Satan tries to deceive us with his lies to prevent us from praising God. In which of the following areas have you fallen for the devil's lies: favoritism, emotions, or self-image (see chapter 6)? How might more praise help you resist Satan's lies and fully submit this area to God?

4. What would change if you turned all the controls of your life over to God—including your intellect, your feelings, and your will?

PRACTICING PRAISE

1. Experience a "sacrifice of praise" (Heb. 13:15) by praying to the Lord the prayer of surrender that is found near the end of chapter 6. If you want, personalize the prayer by adding details from your own life that you want to surrender to the lordship of Christ.

2. This week, during an extended time of prayer and praise, put yourself in a position of humility before the Lord. Kneel before God or fall on your face, prostrate before Him. Maintain that posture during your time of praise. Reflect afterward on how that affected the atmosphere of your praise time.

SMALL GROUP OPTIONS

1. Suggest that group members record in their praise journals how praise is helping them identify and resist the lies of Satan. Ask them to be ready to share their insights during your next meeting.

2. Invite group members to mention an area of pride that is a particular struggle for them. Think about the areas of intellect, feelings, and will. Pray for one another before the meeting ends.

CHAPTER 7

PRAISE FLOWS FROM A THANKFUL HEART

G RATITUDE IS DIFFICULT for many of us because it reminds us that we are totally dependent on God. We can't take credit for anything. As you read chapter 7, think about some things God has done for you that you have never thanked Him for. As they come to mind, stop to thank God for His goodness and provision.

REFLECTING ON PRAISE

1. Expressions of gratitude reveal the condition of our heart. With that in mind, ask yourself:

   + When was the last time you felt genuine gratitude to God for something He provided or something He did for you? How did you express your thanks to Him?

   + When was the last time you thanked God for His limitless love?

   + When was the last time you thanked God for sending Jesus to die on the cross so that you might be saved from the consequences of sin?

2. In your praise journal, make a list of three things you can do, starting today, that will help you cultivate a greater attitude of gratitude.

PRACTICING PRAISE

1. In your praise journal, write down a list of twenty-five things for which you are thankful. Spend time praising and thanking God for each item on your list.

2. Read John 3:13–18 and John 10:10, and then write a thank-you letter to the Lord for giving you both "eternal life" and an abundant life on earth.

3. Write on a note card or small placard the words "Try Thanksgiving." Post it where you will see it every day—and then heed its message.

SMALL GROUP OPTIONS

1. Ask a group member to read Psalm 100 aloud. As the psalm is being read, think about the things you are most thankful for.

2. Have each person write down the top five things for which he or she is most grateful. Then read these blessings aloud to one another. You may want to do this by category—the top five related to family, to the neighborhood, to the community, to the local church, to the workplace, in our country, in our walk with God, and so forth.

3. Ask group members to refer to their praise journal entries related to the previous lesson and tell how praise has helped them identify and resist the lies of Satan.

4. Spend time together thanking God specifically for some of the victories and the blessings you shared with one another.

CHAPTER 8

PRAISE HONORS GOD
FOR WHO HE IS

I F WE'RE NOT experienced in the practice of praise, it's easy to
run out of things to praise God for. But Scripture is filled with
descriptions of God as He reveals Himself to us through His
names, His attributes, and His actions. As you read chapter 8,
seek new ways to praise God for His nature.

REFLECTING ON PRAISE

1. In Revelation 11:18, God is praised as both our rewarder and
   our judge. Do you find it difficult to praise God as the judge of
   your life? If so, why? What steps do you believe God wants you
   to take so you can praise Him freely for being your judge? (See
   Revelation 15:3–4.)

2. Can you identify specific things for which you know God will
   reward you? (See Hebrews 11:6.) Are you reluctant to name them?
   If so, why? Why is it important to identify those things that bring
   God's reward?

PRACTICING PRAISE

1. Write out a statement of praise to God as Elohim, the Most High
   God, the Creator of both the physical and spiritual realms.

2. Write out a statement of praise to God as El Shaddai, God
   Almighty, our Protector and the One who governs all circumstances in our lives.

3. Write out a statement of praise to God as our judge and our rewarder. In these statements be specific and personal. Cite things that pertain directly to your life. You may want to allot a page in your praise journal for each statement of praise. Add to your statements over the coming weeks and months.

SMALL GROUP OPTIONS

1. Share together your response to God as:

   + Elohim, the Most High God, our Creator

   + El Shaddai, the almighty God, the Lord over creation

   + God our judge, whose judgment is just and true

   + God our rewarder, who rewards those who fear Him and who "earnestly seek him" (Heb. 11:6)

2. Ask group members to share their individual praises. Write the combined list on a large tablet or a dry-erase board, and then share a time of prayer in which you praise God as Elohim, El Shaddai, judge, and rewarder.

CHAPTER 9

PRAISE CALLS GOD BY NAME

S TUDYING THE DIFFERENT names God used for Himself helps us understand more about His character. As you read chapter 9, think about times you have seen God act in accordance with each of His names.

REFLECTING ON PRAISE

1. From the following list of God's names, reflect on which name or names is/are most meaningful to you. Choose one of God's names and praise Him for being who He is in your life.

   + Jehovah Jireh, God our Provider

   + Jehovah Rapha, God our Healer

   + Jehovah Nissi, God our Banner

   + Jehovah Mekaddish, God who makes us holy

   + Jehovah Shalom, God our Peace

   + Jehovah Rohi, God our Shepherd

   + Jehovah Tsidkenu, God our Righteousness

   + Jehovah Shammah, God who is present always

2. Identify specific ways in which God has manifested Himself to you. Ask yourself:

   + In what ways has God provided for me as Jehovah Jireh?

- In what ways has God healed me as Jehovah Rapha?

- In what ways has God protected me or led me to victory as Jehovah Nissi?

- In what ways has God made me holy, acting as Jehovah Mekaddish?

- In what ways has God given me His peace as Jehovah Shalom?

- In what ways has God manifested Himself as my Good Shepherd, Jehovah Rohi?

- In what ways has God strengthened me to walk in righteousness as Jehovah Tsidkenu?

- In what ways have I felt God's presence with me "always" as Jehovah Shammah?

PRACTICING PRAISE

1. Using your answers to the above questions, write out a praise statement for each of the Jehovah names of God. You may want to designate an entire page in your praise journal for each name. Add to your praise statement as you recall various incidents or experiences in your life, or as you gain greater insight into the ways in which God has been at work in you and through you.

2. Focus your praise on one name of God each day for the next eight days. Recount the ways in which God has manifested Himself to you as your Creator, Provider, Shepherd, and so forth. Focus your praise on events, experiences, and insights you have had in the last few days. You might begin your praise, "Lord, I praise and thank You that just yesterday You revealed Yourself as Jehovah Tsidkenu, my Righteousness, in these ways..."

SMALL GROUP OPTIONS

1. Have members share the name of Jehovah God that holds the most meaning for them and then explain why.

2. Share a time of prayer in which you praise God for revealing Himself through the eight Jehovah names.

CHAPTER 10

PRAISE INVOLVES GENEROUS GIVING

P RAISE AND GIVING go hand in hand. In chapter 10 the author writes: "Giving can occur without praise, but there cannot be genuine praise without giving." As you read chapter 10, think about your attitude toward giving and whether your giving is linked with genuine praise.

REFLECTING ON PRAISE

1. Think about your giving habits. Why do you give to God? What do you believe your gifts represent to God? What do your gifts represent to you?

2. The author describes three attitudes in giving: the flint-like giver, who gives only after being hammered; the sponge-like giver, who gives only after being squeezed; and the honeycomb-like giver, who gives gladly and generously. Which type of giver are you? Why?

PRACTICING PRAISE

1. Read 2 Corinthians 8:1–5, 7, 9. Consider the sacrificial attitude demonstrated in the generous gift of the Macedonian Christians. Then pray about making a sacrificial offering to the Lord.

2. As you pray about your sacrificial offering, voice to God your acknowledgment that He is the owner of all things in your life.

Ask Him to receive your gift as an expression of praise. Then trust Him with the outcome of your sacrifice.

SMALL GROUP OPTIONS

1. Discuss the ways in which your group study of praise has led to greater generosity or more urgency in your giving.

2. Discuss the impact you believe more praise in your body of believers would have on your church as a whole.

CHAPTER 11

PRAISE DEFEATS THE ENEMY

O NE REASON WE don't experience more victory over temptation is that we are neglecting the praise of God. As you read chapter 11, think about the areas of your life in which you feel powerless. How can praising God open your life to His power?

REFLECTING ON PRAISE

1. Victory over our enemy, Satan, is possible only through the power of God and the sacrifice of Christ on the cross. To help you draw on the power of Christ, ask yourself:

    + Who is the Christ?

    + Who am I in Christ?

2. Read David's words of praise as he went into battle against Goliath (1 Sam. 17:45–47). What spiritual battle are you facing today? In what ways is the Lord leading you to enter that battle with praise on your lips?

3. It is believed that David wrote Psalm 8 after he defeated Goliath. Read the positive affirmations he makes about God in that psalm, then reflect on your daily struggle to speak positive expressions of trust in God. What might you do to increase the level of your positive speech?

PRACTICING PRAISE

1. Identify a major area of concern in your life today. Write out a declaration of war against the devil related to that area of difficulty, struggle, trial, or deprivation. As part of your declaration of war against the enemy of your soul, include these weapons:

   + Write out at least five verses or passages of Scripture that relate to your greatest need.

   + Write out what you believe Jesus has already done to defeat the devil in this area of your life.

2. Once you have completed your declaration of war, voice it! Begin to praise God for the victory He has already accomplished through the shed blood of Christ.

SMALL GROUP OPTIONS

1. Confide in one other group member with an area of personal struggle. Ask that person to pray for you every day this week to experience victory over Satan. Ask that person to check with you next week for a progress report.

2. Offer your prayer support to a group member who is struggling with a particular temptation. Remember to pray daily for God to work in that person's life and praise Him for securing victory over Satan.

CHAPTER 12

PRAISE OVERCOMES NEGATIVE CIRCUMSTANCES

W<small>E NEED TO</small> praise God at all times, and especially during times of personal struggle. Think about God's power to overcome difficulties as you read chapter 12.

REFLECTING ON PRAISE

1. As you think about the past few weeks, write down the three circumstances in your life that trouble you the most.

2. For each circumstance, think of a way to praise God in spite of that circumstance. Then go ahead and praise Him.

3. Read Acts 16:20–40 and reflect on Paul's and Silas' praise to God while they were being held without cause in a jail cell. How did their praise link heaven and earth? What was the outcome of their praise, and whose lives were changed as a result?

4. What blessing are you expecting from God? Do you have scriptural validation for that blessing? Are you already praising God for that blessing?

PRACTICING PRAISE

1. Identify one thing that qualifies as "the desire of your heart." Make sure you identify something that is in keeping with God's plan and purpose for you. Then begin to praise God for His promises in the Bible that He will provide your heart's desire.

2. Offer this same praise to the Lord every day until you receive an answer.

SMALL GROUP OPTIONS

1. Ask group members to share something that they desire for God to do in the life of someone close to them. Claim a promise of God from Scripture that indicates His will in the matter.

2. Praise God as a group for His promises to work in the lives of those you are praying for.

CHAPTER 13

PRAISE EMPOWERS PRAYER AND MINISTRY

IF YOUR PRAYER life lacks power or if your ministry lacks boldness, perhaps you're not investing enough of your life in praise. As you read chapter 13, think about how you'd like God to work in your prayer life and through you in the lives of others.

REFLECTING ON PRAISE

1. The author makes the statement that "praise energizes our faith." Reflect on that statement, and then write in your praise journal how praising God over the past few weeks has activated and strengthened your trust in Him.

2. In what way is the Lord leading you to greater service or an expanded ministry? Are you already praising the Lord for the lives that will be impacted by the Holy Spirit as He works through you?

3. After reflecting on each of the following statements, write down an example of one way you have seen this become reality in your own life.

   + Praise empowers our prayer.

   + Praise energizes our faith.

   + Praise emboldens our ministry to others.

+ Praise builds on itself. (The more we praise God, the more we want to praise Him.)

PRACTICING PRAISE

1. Write out a praise statement for your spouse and for each of your children. If you are not married or do not have children, write out a praise statement for a close friend, a niece or nephew, a godchild, or another person who is close to you. Praise God for the way He has worked in the life of this person, bringing blessing, victory, peace, healing, and so forth.

2. Write out a praise statement for your pastor.

SMALL GROUP OPTIONS

1. As a group, create a "composite" statement of praise to God for working in your lives in the following areas:

+ Drawing near to you

+ Changing you

+ Drawing out your emotions

+ Calling you to bear witness

+ Overcoming pride

+ Prompting thankfulness and generous giving

+ Overcoming Satan's lies and temptations

+ Overcoming negative circumstances

+ Empowering prayer and ministry

Make sure each member of the group shares at least one item of praise from his or her own life. Write the combined list on a large tablet or a dry-erase board, then share a time of prayer in which you praise God for His work in your lives.

NOTES

INTRODUCTION

1. C. S. Lewis, *Reflections on the Psalms* (New York: Harcourt, 1958), 90–91.
2. Lewis, *Reflections on the Psalms*, 95, 97.

CHAPTER 1

1. "Westminster Catechism," Britannica, accessed May 25, 2021, https://www.britannica.com/topic/Westminster-Catechism.
2. C. S. Lewis, *The Problem of Pain* (New York: Macmillan, 1962), 150.

CHAPTER 2

1. Chad Walsh, *Early Christians of the 21st Century* (New York: Harper & Brothers, 1950), 11.
2. Attributed to Jack Taylor, at InfoSearch Pro Version 4.21e, *The Communicator's Companion* (Dallas: The Computer Assistant, December 1998), 9197.

CHAPTER 5

1. Elizabeth Knowles, ed., *The Oxford Dictionary of Phrase, Saying and Quotation* (New York: Oxford University Press, 1997), 152.

CHAPTER 6

1. Joseph S. Carroll, *How to Worship Jesus Christ* (Chicago: Moody Press, 1991), 49.

CHAPTER 7

1. "Try Thanksgiving," Our Daily Bread, accessed July 5, 2021, https://odb.org/US/2000/11/22/try-thanksgiving.

CHAPTER 10

1. Attributed to John R. Mott, at InfoSearch Pro Version 4.21e, *The Communicator's Companion* (Dallas: The Computer Assistant, December 1998), 10213.
2. Attributed to Clovis Chapel, at InfoSearch, 4322.

CHAPTER 11

1. Attributed to Diogenes Laertius, in John Bartlett, *Familiar Quotations*, 10th ed. (Boston: Little Brown, 1919), http://www.Bartleby.com, 2000, 9151.

2. Attributed to Blaise Pascal, in Bartlett, *Familiar Quotations*, 9569.
3. Attributed to Mark Twain, at InfoSearch Pro Version 4.21e, *The Communicator's Companion* (Dallas: The Computer Assistant, December 1998), 3345.

CHAPTER 13

1. Attributed to R. A. Torrey, at InfoSearch Pro Version 4.21e, *The Communicator's Companion* (Dallas: The Computer Assistant, December 1998), 8333.
2. For more on the Lord's Prayer, I encourage you to read my book *The Prayer That God Answers* (Nashville: Thomas Nelson, 2000).

Connect with
Dr. Michael Youssef!

Follow Dr. Youssef for life-giving truth, behind-the-scenes ministry updates, and much more.

MichaelYoussef.com

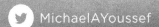 MichaelAYoussef

 Michael A. Youssef

Discover More
from Michael Youssef and
Leading The Way